ANTHROPOLOGICAL PAPERS OF
THE UNIVERSITY OF ARIZONA
NUMBER 24

POPULATION, CONTACT, AND CLIMATE IN THE NEW MEXICAN PUEBLOS

EZRA B. W. ZUBROW

THE UNIVERSITY OF ARIZONA PRESS
TUCSON, ARIZONA 1974

About the Author . . .

EZRA ZUBROW'S interest in demography as it relates to cultural process has led him into numerous research projects and scholarly conclaves focusing on that theme. In 1973 he was chairman of a conference on demographic structure and cultural process at the School of American Research in Santa Fe, New Mexico. In 1971 he completed his dissertation on "A Southwestern Test of a Model of Population Dynamics." An archaeologist as well, Zubrow has done fieldwork at several locations in the Rocky Mountain West and Southwest and in the Middle East and Mexico. In 1972 and 1973, he was a director of Stanford University's project with the Mexican government on Prehistoric Regionalization, at Guanajuato, Mexico, underlining his primary interest in testing ecological, demographic, and economic models over long time spans. Zubrow holds a B.A. in anthropology from Harvard and advanced degrees from the University of Arizona. In 1971 he joined the faculty at Stanford University.

THE UNIVERSITY OF ARIZONA PRESS

CONTENTS

ILLUSTRATIONS

TABLES

ACKNOWLEDGMENTS

There are numerous people whose criticism and help should be recognized in the development of this book from an M.A. thesis. It should be noted also that since 1969 when this was written, more data have become available. The 1970 census and some of the climatic data refined by the later work of Harold Fritts would have been welcome additions.

I must thank Jane Underwood, William Longacre, and the late Edward Dozier, who patiently reviewed, criticized, and made constructive suggestions throughout the entire study. Raymond Thompson was instrumental in obtaining an NDEA fellowship, without which my graduate education would have been far more difficult. In addition, his editorial suggestions were invaluable.

I would like to thank Harold Fritts, William J. Robinson, and the staff of the Laboratory of Tree-Ring Research for their help in explaining their techniques. David Adam cheerfully helped me through the computer programming of the polynomial regression, and answered innumerable questions about the rest of the programming.

I owe a large debt to the Strategic Air Command of the United States Air Force and particularly to Colonel Waters and Lieutenant Charles Hardilek, who not only donated their time, but made available resources which were crucial to the latter part of this study.

The Geography Department of the University of Arizona not only allowed me to use its facilities through the courtesy of Thomas F. Saarinen, but Richard Reeves, their cartographer, explained to me the fundamentals of photo-interpretation and the use of the Compensating Polar Planimeter.

The line illustrations were executed by Patricia Mail, who was able miraculously to make my rough sketches into professional illustrations. Similarly, Hazel Gillie patiently typed the final drafts of this work.

Additionally, I owe a debt to my fellow students in the Department of Anthropology, whose ideas and friendship have been stimulating during my graduate education.

I am particularly grateful to Paul S. Martin, Mark Leone, Frederick Plog, my other colleagues, and students of the Southwestern Archaeological Expedition of the Field Museum of Natural History for advice, guidance, and encouragement covering all aspects of the general paradigm under which this study was attempted. The University of Arizona Press is also to be thanked for bringing about publication.

Finally, I wish to thank Marcia, Anne, and Reuben Zubrow, to whom this book is dedicated.

E. B. W. Zubrow

CHAPTER 1
THEORIES AND CONCEPTS

Anthropologists in our times have become cognizant of the importance of examining the mutual articulation of environment and culture. Already, a respectable history of anthropological-ecological studies exists in the four sub-disciplines. In physical anthropology, the differentiation of races and problems in human evolution has acquired an ecological slant through the studies of Birdsell (1953) and Newman (1953). In archaeology, Clark (1952) has utilized aspects of plant and animal ecology to develop his interpretation of European prehistoric development. Flannery and Coe have made ecological relationships the primary focus for their explanations of the development of agriculture in the Middle East and Mesoamerica (Flannery and Coe 1964; Flannery 1965). This interest has blossomed into whole volumes, such as Ucko and Dimbleby's (1969) *The Domestication and Exploitation of Plants and Animals.* After Kroeber's (1939) and Steward's (1938) critical studies, Bennett's prediction (1944) that there would be a growing trend of attention to ecological studies in ethnography and ethnology was quickly substantiated by Hallowell (1949), Thompson (1949), Birdsell (1953), and Meggers (1954). In linguistics, several aspects of the semantic relativity of environmental perception have become major foci for study, for example, botany (Conklin 1955), color (Conklin 1964), property (Goodenough 1964), and disease (Frake 1964). These studies have increased so rapidly in the late fifties and sixties that it would be cumbersome as well as a major bibliographic exercise to list them all here. Among the later articles are Yengoyan (1968), Birdsell (1968), and Sanders (1968).

At the theoretical level, Julian Steward (1938, 1955), Leslie White (1943, 1959), and Marshall Sahlins (1958) have led in reassessing the role that natural environment has played in an individual culture. For example:

Every cultural system exists in a natural habitat, a collection of flora, fauna, topography. . . . And every culture is of course affected by these environmental factors. But the relationship between culture and environment is not a one to one correlation. . . . Environments vary, and their influence and effect upon culture varies likewise (White 1959: 50-51).

A simple truism underlies the concept of adaptive variation: that exploitation of the energy resources of the natural world for the purpose of sustaining human life is a requirement which all cultures must meet. With this in mind, attention is focused on the environment in which a society is articulated with the natural world. The interaction of a particular technological system with a given environment is the basic adaptation of a culture. It is held that the basic adaptation effected by any culture will be reflected in the social structure, because of the organizational requirements of manipulating the technology and distributing life-sustaining goods. And if cultures are in any way cohesive wholes, it is expectable that corresponding ideological sanctions of the prevailing social and technological conditions will be found (Sahlins 1958: 247).

It is clear from these studies that human populations, unlike floral or faunal populations, are not only facilitated by culture in adapting to their environment, but that the study of these adaptations is complicated by the addition of the cultural variable. A totally synthetic theory of culture (although suited as a theory of culture) is operationally difficult to apply to the analysis of interdependent factors with which ecology must deal. As Hallowell (1949) and Steward (1955) noted, the analytical approach to human ecology must isolate variables from the systems of culture and ecology, and study them independently and in relation to each other. Thus, the analysis in this study is not concerned with culture as an undifferentiated totality, but with aspects of culture as they are involved with the process of adaptation.

A Model for Human Ecology

For heuristic purposes a simplified model of the human ecology has been suggested by Duncan (1959). It consists of four mutually articulated categories: environment, organization, technology, and population (Fig. 1). As a working definition of *environment* I suggest the following: the aggregate of all non-human external conditions which influence or modify the existence of the population. These conditions include natural phenomena such as topography, climate and hydrology; botanical phenomena such as ground cover, trees (at the macro-level), and

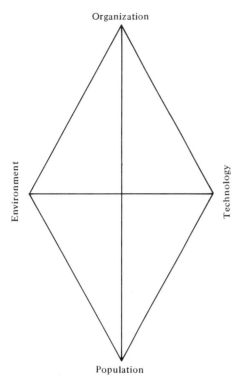

Organization

Environment

Technology

Population

Fig. 1. A Simplified Model for Human Ecology (Adapted from Duncan 1959).

algae (at the micro-level); and zoological phenomena of all sizes. At the population level of analysis, the term is relativistic since the environment for one population is not the environment for another. Different natural, biological, and zoological forces impinge upon each population. Although descriptively the environment may be delineated only with regard to a particular population, ecologists have shown the existence of regularities common to all populations and their environments.

Under *organization* one may subsume a variety of social and ideological subsystems, including social structure, language, and religion. I am using the term *organization* to specify all the cultural phenomena which allow a human population to maintain its corporate non-technological identity.

The reason for considering *technology* a separate category rather than a subsystem of *organization* is that one of the major connections between environment and population is through the subsistence base, the production of which is a primary function of technology. An operational definition of *technology,* therefore, would be the systematic knowledge and culturally shaped material artifacts which allow men

to cope with their environment and each other in both constructive and destructive ways.

Following Villee (1962), who defines a *population* as a group of organisms of the same species occupying a given area, we may define a *human population* ecologically as the members of *Homo sapiens* within the area bounded by a biotic community. Human populations, similar to all biological populations, have characteristics which are the function of the whole group and not of individuals, such as growth and dispersion rates, birth and death rates, population size and density, biotic potential, and age distribution.

Although man culturally has freed himself to an extent from his unmodified environment, he is bound by physiological toleration to certain biological dictates. He is also limited in his role in the biotic community by other populations of organisms with which he interacts and trades influence. The combined ecological and anthropological framework outlined since World War II has not only broached a new series of problems, but has developed more refined methods of evolving them. This study will isolate and examine in detail a series of population and environmental variables for the New Mexican Pueblos. In order to explain the results, however, it will be necessary to utilize organizational and technological considerations as well as environmental and population factors.

Isolation of the Population Variables

An advantage of isolating population variables is that the population concept is not only modern (Simpson 1957), but it has wide ramifications and applications throughout many branches of science (Boulding 1950). It is easier to relate the theory of several disciplines in an interdisciplinary approach when a common unit exists. Within some of the natural sciences (ecology, zoology, and physical anthropology) and social sciences (demography, cultural anthropology, and economics), the generic concept "population" is the common focus for viewing a universe of phenomena. Although the phenomena comprise recognizable individual elements, the generic concept is concerned with such group attributes as number, composition, distribution, and change. Secondly, this concept is highly amenable to quantitative analysis, since in its most abstract sense the concept was developed in statistical "renewal" and "sampling" theory. The former refers to deterministic and stochastic models of generalized accretion and depletion. The latter was developed to meet the need for a criteria of representativeness by means of which rigorous inferences about the composition and dynamics of a population may be based upon observations of a small percentage of that population.

Two of the population variables which will be isolated are size and growth. Several theoretical models to explain these variations have been developed; probably the most famous was conceived by the economist Malthus. His *Essay on Population*, published in 1798, suggests that population when unchecked will increase geometrically due to the inherent "attraction between the sexes." However, sustenance increases only in an arithmetic ratio, or as an anonymous writer succinctly stated:

To get land's fruit in quantity,
Takes jolts of labor ever more,
Hence food will grow like one, two, three,. . .
While numbers grow like one, two, four,. . .
(From the "Song of Malthus: A Ballad of Diminishing Returns")

Thus, population increases until the limit placed by the subsistence base is reached. This limit is enforced through the "positive checks" of famine, disease, and war unless man utilizes what Malthus termed the "preventive checks": deferred marriage and celibacy.

Time has shown major errors in his theory; first and least important, the ratios were in error. Malthus, himself, tacitly admitted his mistake, and in the second edition (1803) of the *Essay* he placed far less emphasis on the ratios. Second, his hypothesis that each advance in technology is absorbed by a consequent increase in population, which prevents in turn any increase in the standard of living, was disproved by the industrial revolution. As an empirical generalization, it was valid for most of the world through the 1760s. As a general law, it collapsed due to the fallacious assumption that increases in production could never exceed increases in population. Malthus had underestimated man's technological ingenuity and almost unlimited capacity to move both himself and his goods. However, one must examine the more recent formulations of the Malthusian doctrine before accepting the following negative conclusion:

. . .The major contribution of such formulations has been to provide a general framework for the discussion of problems of the adjustment of population to resources and policy questions related thereto. They have not been notably helpful in identifying the immediate factors governing population changes, predicting rates of growth or patterns of movement in the short run, or explaining the various empirical regularities discovered in population research (Duncan and Hauser 1959: 13).

The neo-Malthusians (e.g., Peabody and Boulding) have noted that it took an industrial revolution to disprove Malthus. Thus, in conservative agricultural or underdeveloped areas (such as the Pueblos) where the industrial revolution has not changed the potential for production by several quantum leaps, the doctrine of Malthus is thought still to apply. Although the concept of standard of living stability is rejected, the conclusion that population growth is a correlate of technological change is viable under pre-industrial conditions. If the economic forces are somewhat inevitable, as certain members of that "dismal" science have suggested, a modern ecological model is apropos. The Malthusian ratios are replaced by population pressure in a series of organized, spatially differentiated ecosystems, each with its own level of consumption expectations based on food chains with internal and external ecological connections.

A second model developed from attempts in the United States to test empirically the Malthusian and neo-Malthusian doctrine. The theory of growth cycles and transition is a combination of "population pressure" with mathematical analysis. Pearl (1925) suggested that population grew not at a constant but a variable rate. Similar to Toynbee in utilizing the growth curve of biological organisms as a template, he claimed:

The long run tendency of population growth can be represented by a curve which starting from a previously established stationary level, representing the supporting capacity of its region at the prevailing level of culture, productive technique, and the standard of living—rises at first slowly, then at an increasing rate, finally leveling out as the curve approaches an upper asymptote which represents the supporting capacity of the environment at the last stage (requoted from Lorimer 1963: 297).

The mathematical curve which describes this growth cycle is called the "logistic curve" $P=K/(1+e^{a+bx})$, and was suggested by P. F. Verhulst in 1845. The crucial factor is spatial density, and Pearl's experiments on fruit flies gave empirical validation to his theory (Fig. 2A)

Although the logistic curve was never refuted in a critical attack, it was replaced by transition theory due to its inaccurate predictions toward the end of the curve, which is shaped like an elongated "s." Its weakness was the assumption of initial stationary growth rates and its empirical failure to find stable populations at the "upper asymptote." Dorn (1950) tested the curve built from 1790-1940, and found the prediction for 1950 in significant error. Notestein (1945), building on Willcox (1931), noted that the gap caused by an initial decrease in deaths is closed and a new equilibrium is reached when a similar decline in fertility takes place. This transition between points of dynamic equilibrium shows that the logistic curve for growth may be stimulated by an increase in birth rate or a decrease in death rate, and

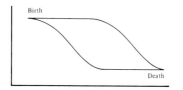

2A The result of Pearl's Logistic Growth Cycle

2B Probable Cycle of Births and Deaths

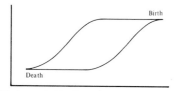

2C Improbable Cycle of Births and Deaths

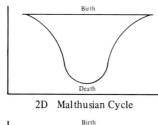

2D Malthusian Cycle

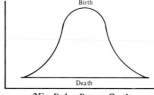

2E Baby Boom Cycle

Fig. 2.   The Logistic Growth Cycle
A. Result of Pearl's Logistic Growth Cycle
B-E. Transitional Growth Curves Resulting in the Logistic Curve

terminated (Fig. 2B) either by a decreased birth rate or an increased death rate (Cowgill 1949).

Vance claims the theory fills the requirements of a high level analysis. It is dynamic rather than static, and takes into account culture contact and social interaction. However, it will be shown later in this study that the Pueblo data substantiate Duncan and Hauser's criticism.

As concerns explanation and especially prediction, however, transition theory. . .has succeeded only in suggesting certain major complexes of poorly defined influences on components of population change. . . . The influences on population growth that it postulates are closely bound up with the particular historical circumstance of population growth in Western countries (1959: 14).

A similiar criticism is valid for Gini's (1930) "parabolic curve."

Although less well known outside of actuarial and demographic circles, analytical theory has a history longer than the Malthusian theory. It developed in three major steps: 1) the development of life tables, 2) the recognition of the relation of a closed population with constant vital rates to its mortality schedule and rate of increase, and 3) the development of the systematic interrelationships between births, deaths, sex, and age structure. In the 1690s, Halley, an astronomer, first produced the modern life tables, which later became known as examples of "stationary populations" (Lorimer 1959), for the number of births equaled the number of deaths.

In the 1760s Euler, a Swiss mathematician, made the concept dynamic by showing that age distribution could be determined by age-specific mortality and fertility rates, whether the closed population was increasing, decreasing, or stationary. Finally, Lotka, in 1926, developed a complete general theory of the interrelationships of primary biological processes, including determinants of age and sex, if one assumed constant age-sex-specific mortality rates and fertility rates, and a constant sex ratio at birth.

Johnston (1966: 180) attempted to apply Lotka's models to the Navajo population with data similar to those available for the Pueblos. He explains the failure of these models as follows:

In the first place, the basic mortality rates from which the several United Nations model life tables were developed are heavily weighted by age-specific mortality levels reported among European countries since 1920. One can certainly question the degree to which these largely European rates would pertain to the members of a population such as the Navaho, whose entire mode and condition of life are so different. Second, the selection of the most appropriate model or group of models to represent a specific population at a particular time in its development is confronted with great difficulties, when we lack reliable information on precisely those values which we need in guiding our selection. . .[that is]. . .fairly precise knowledge of the infant or early childhood mortality.

Isolation of Environmental Variables

Ecology, since it is the study of the relation of animals and plants to their environment, has the initial task of examining those environmental factors that control the distribution, size, and growth of populations (Broughey 1968). Odum (1953) lists the following limiting factors which act in combination: 1) temperature, 2) radiation and light, 3) water, 4) temperature and moisture acting together, 5) microclimates, 6) atmospheric gases and biogenic salts, 7) currents and pressures, 8) soil, and 9) fire. This concept of limiting factors is based upon two laws: Lieberg's law of the minimum and Shelford's law of tolerance. In combined form, Broughey (1968: 2,3) paraphrases them thus:

. . .the establishment of a particular organism in a given area is dependent upon the availability of the necessary elements in the required minimum quantity and the functioning of initial physical factors at the required minimal level, combined with the occurrence of these elements and the operation of these factors within the tolerance limits of the organism.

The environmental factors which will be isolated in this study are solely climatic, with a strong emphasis on temperature and moisture. The rationale for isolating climatic factors is twofold. They have been the most widely studied of the ecologically limiting factors (Broughey 1968), and there exist considerable detailed data for the Rio Grande area over a long temporal span (Fritts 1965).

In addition to utilizing the concept of limiting factors, I will employ the concepts of *food chains* and *carrying capacity,* which were also developed in ecology. Odum (1953: 68) defines a *food chain* as:

The transfer of food energy from the source in plants through a series of organisms with repeated eating and being eaten is referred to as the food chain. . . . The number of steps or links in a sequence is limited, usually to four or five. The shorter the food chain. . .the greater the protoplasm mass or biomass that can be supported with a given basic source of potential food energy.

Carrying capacity is the maximum number of organisms or amounts of biomass which can maintain themselves indefinitely in an area: in other words, a homeostatic equilibrium point. This point is homeostatic in that there is a tendency toward the maintenance of a state of balance between opposite forces or processes which will result in a diminishing net change or a stable constant. It is dynamic in that the point at which the state of balance exists may change over time and space.

What are the two opposing forces which determine the equilibrium? On the one hand, Liebig's extended law (Broughey 1968: 2) states that population size is determined by maxima and minima of specific resources. On the other hand, the "prime dynamic mover" appears to be reproduction. A population will tend to keep reproducing and growing in size until reaching an ultimate limit determined by the supply of nutrients and energy. A change in the supply results in a change in the carrying capacity with a consequent growth or decrease of the biomass, until a new equilibrium is reached. Letter A of Figure 3 denotes a carrying capacity equilibrium point. If a change in the resource curves takes place from Resource 1 to Resource 2, there results a disequilibrium, with resources greater than population. We would expect the biomass or population to grow along the population curve until a new equilibrium

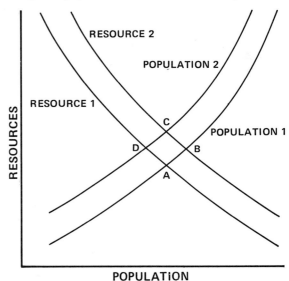

Fig. 3. Carrying Capacity as a Dynamic Equilibrium System. *Note:* **Resource 1 and Resource 2 refer to iso-resource curves (or resource levels) in which resources plus population equal an energy or biomass constant.**

point B is reached. Similarly, one may predict what would happen in the other cases: a decrease in the resource curve or an increase or decrease in the population curve.

Such neo-Malthusian models have both advantages and disadvantages. The primary advantages are: 1) given the initial conditions, one may predict the expected consequences; and 2) one may quantify both initial conditions and expected results. The primary disadvantage of this type of neo-Malthusian model building is that contemporary demographic and ecological data do not lend themselves to testing the model, because the time span for which data exists is too short in relation to long term ecological processes. Secondarily, modern technological development with its concomitant diversity of resources, complex trade patterns, and ease of mobility, complicates the data to the point that it is necessary to utilize factor and discriminant analyses to remove masking data patterns and variables.

Ethnohistory is thus in a unique position to evaluate this type of model. Its data span long periods of time, and some of the societies it considers have not developed the complex networks of resource, trade systems, and technologies which distinguish modern industrial nation states. As presented, the model is oversimplified. A mathematically more sophisticated and conceptually more complete version of this model may be found in "Carrying Capacity and Dynamic Equilibrium in the Prehistoric Southwest" (Zubrow 1971a) and in *A Southwestern Test of an Anthropological Model of Population Dynamics* (Zubrow 1971b). The former includes a more complete graphic analysis, showing the implications of migration and multiple microhabitats. The latter presents a mathematical simulation of the model, allows for cultural limitations below the energy-resource limits, and compares simulated results to actual prehistoric demographic data.

CHAPTER 2

A BRIEF HISTORY, THE ALTERNATIVE HYPOTHESES, AND THE DATA

A Brief History

The archaeological period which corresponds approximately to the pre-contact period for the Rio Grande Pueblos is Pueblo IV (A.D. 1300-1600). Although the period has been called "regressive" and "retractive" (Willey 1966), a label less connotatively negative would be better since there was no general decline in terms of material culture. On the other hand, technological innovations from an economic viewpoint were minor. Reed (1964) lists only three innovations for the whole three-hundred-year period:

1. The use of metallic glaze paint which spread from East-Central Arizona to the Rio Grande.

2. The appearance of Sikyatki polychrome pottery in the Hopi area.

3. The change in the settlement pattern to the formal arrangement of a town around the plaza.

During the early part of the period, there was an archaeologically documented trend toward the congregation of the population into larger but fewer towns. Thus, the total area of Anasazi occupation shrank. This trend resulted (Willey 1966: 211):

[in] ... the northern regions [being] abandoned during the late years of the 13th century, leaving the Anasazi concentrated on the Little Colorado and the Northern Rio Grande. It was in these locations that the Spanish found the Pueblos in the 16th century.

Spanish contact began with Coronado's visit to the Rio Grande, 1540-42, but colonization and missionization did not begin until 1598 with Oñate's expedition. The "encomienda" system of the early contact period not only used the Indians as effective serfs, but made the Franciscan missionaries responsible for persecution of large numbers of Pueblo Indians who attempted to retain their native religion (Dozier 1967). After the Pueblo Revolt (1680-93), the Pueblos followed a course of passive resistance and conservatism under Spanish, Mexican, and U.S. rule. Yielding when forced to, they nevertheless maintained their ideological and social institutions to a

degree that their total culture in the 20th century is still intact, although severely modified by the Europeans. This process of "compartmentalization" (Dozier 1961) has resulted in a partially acculturated society, conserving the valued traditional religious and social orientation, but accepting the less valued technological innovations from the dominant society.

...thus, the Pueblos continue to exist as social and cultural enclaves surrounded by the dominant Anglo-American society and culture. They have improved health conditions and accommodated to the economy and educational requirements of the dominant society, but within the confines of their communities they cling tenaciously to their own language and ceremonial organization (Dozier 1967: 30).

The First Hypothesis

Against this background of definitions and theoretical models, and the brief history presented above, the first hypothesis may be tested. In simplified form it is as follows: As population contact increases, the importance of climate (rainfall and temperature) in determining the parameters of Pueblo population decreases. Behind this hypothesis lies an argument based upon the simplifying assumptions of the neo-Malthusian model and ecological concepts. As previously stated, the total biomass of organisms increases until the carrying capacity is reached. If I make the operating assumption that man's physiological biomass is relatively constant, an increase in human biomass is caused primarily by increased numbers. Prior to contact, the Pueblos had a successful adaptation to their environment over a long period of time (approximately 300 years) with a stable technology. They were thus close to the population specific size — that is, at equilibrium. During the pre-contact period, changes in the limiting factors would probably cause changes in population.

With the introduction of contact, however, there is gradual technological change. For example, the Spanish introduced the metal plow and hoe, and European crops such as grapes, peaches, wheat, and barley. From the neo-Malthusian model we would expect that, with technological change, there will be an increase of population with no change in the standard of living. Therefore, until the carrying capacity is reached, the importance of the limiting factors is minimized (Fig. 3). Although one might ask whether the opposite could not have occurred, that is, an increase in the standard of living with population size remaining constant, there is no historical evidence of an increase in the standard of living (Spicer 1962).

It is difficult to devise diachronically accurate measures of contact and environment, since both are determined by and composed of multiple factors. Thus, I have restricted myself to measuring Pueblo population, population contact, and a combined climatic limiting factor composed of temperature and rainfall. The three variables may be interrelated in seven additional ways as well as in our primary hypothesis. It is possible to state all eight hypotheses in symbolic form, as follows:

Hypothesis 1. $PC\uparrow\ \alpha$ corr $(NP\uparrow\ CL)\uparrow$
Hypothesis 2. $PC\uparrow\ \alpha$ corr $(NP\uparrow\ CL)\downarrow$
Hypothesis 3. $PC\uparrow\ \alpha$ corr $(NP\downarrow\ CL)\uparrow$
Hypothesis 4. $PC\uparrow\ \alpha$ corr $(NP\downarrow\ CL)\downarrow$
Hypothesis 5. $PC\downarrow\ \alpha$ corr $(NP\uparrow\ CL)\uparrow$
Hypothesis 6. $PC\downarrow\ \alpha$ corr $(NP\uparrow\ CL)\downarrow$
Hypothesis 7. $PC\downarrow\ \alpha$ corr $(NP\downarrow\ CL)\uparrow$
Hypothesis 8. $PC\downarrow\ \alpha$ corr $(NP\downarrow\ CL)\downarrow$

where:

> $\uparrow$ = increases
> $\downarrow$ = decreases
> corr = correlation
> NP = native Rio Grande Pueblo population
> Cl = Climate
> PC = Population Contact
> α = direct variation

Or, restated in verbal terms, the hypotheses state:

Hypothesis 1. As population contact increases, the correlation between an increasing native population and climate increases.

Hypothesis 2. As population contact increases, the correlation between an increasing native population and climate decreases.

Hypothesis 3. As population contact increases, the correlation between a decreasing native population and climate increases.

Hypothesis 4. As population contact increases, the correlation between a decreasing native population and climate decreases.

Hypothesis 5. As population contact decreases, the correlation between an increasing native population and climate increases.

Hypothesis 6. As population contact decreases, the correlation between an increasing native population and climate decreases.

Hypothesis 7. As population contact decreases, the correlation between a decreasing native population and climate increases.

Hypothesis 8. As population contact decreases, the correlation between a decreasing native population and climate decreases.

Determination of the Climatic Variable

In July 1965 Professor Fritts published an article entitled "Tree-Ring Evidence for Climatic Changes in Western North America." It was the culmination of work in dendroclimatology that began in 1956 with Edward Schulman's book *Dendroclimatic Changes in Semiarid America.* Fritts' article suggests a model for the physiological relationships causing ring-width growth to correlate with variations in climate. On the basis of this model, Fritts quantified the relationships between climatic factors and fluctuations in dated tree-ring widths. This method was tested against independent climatic data collected by various meteorological stations of the United States Weather Bureau during the last 50 years; the index proves to be highly reliable.

...the variations in tree-ring widths from four southwestern conifers clearly relate to variations in climatic parameters. There is consistent, direct relationship of ring widths with precipitation and an inverse relationship with temperature. The latter is less important, and in many cases, temperature appears to influence growth only if moisture is present in the soil.... Narrow rings in Douglas fir and Ponderosa pine imply low precipitation and high temperatures throughout the entire year, with a somewhat greater weight placed on the climate of autumn, winter, and spring. A narrow ring in Pinyon pine implies a dry warm previous autumn, winter, and spring and a hot June or July. A narrow ring in Bristlecone pine implies a dry, warm climate during the year with the greatest weight placed on the spring, summer, and autumn periods. [Fritts 1965: 426]

Professor Fritts calculated these indices for ten-year periods on the basis of 26 tree-ring chronologies from western North America which he published in the form of a table.

How is this index determined? The years 1651 through 1920 were common to all 26 chronologies. Therefore, this period was chosen as a "standard interval." The mean and standard deviation for the indices were calculated for this "standard interval." Then for the entire length of the chronology, mean indices were calculated for staggered ten-year periods (for example, 1701-10, 1706-15, 1711-20, 1716-25). Each ten-year mean is converted to a relative departure by subtracting the mean and dividing by the standard deviation of the chronology during the 270-year standard interval. The relative departure is then the published index which reflects climate.

In order to see further ramifications, this index may be examined with a more mathematical approach. The tree-ring widths are points through which an irregular curve may be drawn; this curve corresponds to the growth pattern. A smooth curve may then be fitted to the growth pattern of the tree by means of multiple regression techniques.

The hiatus value may be defined as the ring-width measurement divided by the smooth curve value at that point.

$$\frac{\text{ring-width value}}{\text{curve value}} = \text{hiatus value}$$

Fritts calculates the mean and standard deviations of the hiatus values in a long standard interval (270 years) and the mean of the hiatus values in a shorter period (10 years) and expresses the difference between the means in terms of the number of standard deviations. This value is the relative departure for the period, which can be calculated for periods not within the standard interval. The interval is used only to derive a standard deviation and mean hiatus value comparable for all chronologies, not to set limits on the periods to be analyzed.

Relative departure =

$$\frac{(\text{mean hiatus value of period}) - (\text{mean hiatus value of the standard interval})}{(\text{standard deviation of the standard interval})}$$

Or in symbolic form, the relative departure for the chronology is:

$$\text{R.D.} = \frac{\dfrac{\sum\limits_{p=1}^{L} x_p}{L} - \dfrac{\sum\limits_{i=1}^{n} x_i}{n}}{\sqrt{\dfrac{\sum\limits_{i=1}^{n} x_i^2 - \left(\sum\limits_{i=1}^{n} x_i\right)^2 \Big/ n}{n-1}}}$$

where:

x = the hiatus value
p = the years of the period
i = the years of the standard interval
L = the length of the period
n = the length of the standard interval

Table 1 presents the relative departures for the Rio Grande and Navajo areas. A negative relative departure corresponds to a period of drought and high temperature at a particular location; a positive relative departure is indicative of a period of moisture and lower temperature. Since the relative departures are parametric and standardized for all chronologies, it is possible to make individual comparisons. First, one can rank climatic conditions across space. If one compares station seven to station ten in 1681-90, the relative departures are +.33 and +.22 respectively. Since +.33 is greater than +.22, station seven is cooler and moister than station ten, and both are cooler and moister than the average for the standard interval (both are greater than 0.0). Second, one may compare climatic conditions temporally at the same location. In 1751-60 station seven had a relative departure of -.31; in 1756-65, -.05. This difference of +.26 is indicative of a change from a dry hot climate towards a moister cooler one within a ten-year span. Finally, if one wishes to compare two areas either geographically or temporally distinguished, it is possible to compare average values meaningfully. For example, the average relative departure for the first half of the 17th century is +.36; for the second half, it is -.11 at station seven. Needless to say, this difference represents a considerable climatic change from cool moist to dry hot.

It is important to remember that these relative departures are not "absolute" climatology; instead,

TABLE 1
Relative Departures for Rio Grande Valley, 1551-1955
Through Time*

Time Interval	Relative Departure at Station 7	Time Interval	Relative Departure at Station 7
1551-1560	.47	1751-1760	-.31
1556-1565	-.22	1756-1765	-.05
1561-1570	-.63	1761-1770	.54
1566-1575	-.74	1766-1775	.32
1571-1580	-.83	1771-1780	-.23
1576-1585	-1.31	1776-1785	-.15
1581-1590	-1.15	1781-1790	-.24
1586-1595	-.06	1786-1795	.12
1591-1600	.37	1791-1800	.47
1596-1605	.22	1796-1805	-.15
1601-1610	.14	1801-1810	-.47
1605-1615	.46	1806-1815	-.07
1611-1620	.61	1811-1820	-.13
1616-1625	.24	1816-1825	-.75
1621-1630	.20	1821-1830	-.07
1626-1635	.74	1826-1835	.80
1631-1640	.72	1831-1840	.85
1636-1645	.05	1836-1845	.26
1641-1650	-.01	1841-1850	-.43
1646-1655	.42	1846-1855	-.38
1651-1660	.32	1851-1860	.10
1656-1665	.23	1856-1865	-.39
1661-1670	-.34	1861-1870	-.28
1666-1675	-.42	1866-1875	.33
1671-1680	.12	1871-1880	-.20
1676-1685	-.50	1876-1885	-.04
1681-1690	-.33	1881-1890	.39
1686-1695	.44	1886-1895	.10
1691-1700	-.13	1891-1900	-.29
1696-1705	-.45	1896-1905	-.56
1701-1710	-.03	1901-1910	-.11
1706-1715	.23	1906-1915	.73
1711-1720	.12	1911-1920	1.11
1716-1725	.27	1916-1925	.51
1721-1730	.26	1921-1930	.29
1726-1735	-.11	1926-1935	
1731-1740	-.47	1931-1940	
1736-1745	-.53	1936-1945	
1741-1750	-.22	1941-1950	
1746-1755	-.20	1946-1955	

*Abstracted from Fritts

they represent "relative" climatology. Relative departures will not tell us the exact amount of rainfall or the temperature. What they will tell is whether the climate is warmer, dryer, colder, or damper at one station than at another, or how it has changed over time. Summarizing the data from the entire Western United States, one may note widespread drought in 1576-90, 1626-35, 1776-85, 1841-50, 1871-80, 1931-50. Periods of "better than average" moisture occurred in 1611-25, 1641-50, 1741-55, 1826-40, 1906-20. The moist periods of 1611-25 and 1906-20 were the most geographically widespread and the most markedly above average.

Determination of the Population Variable

The population variable is based upon historical and contemporary sources. The data are derived from:

H. H. Bancroft's *The History of New Mexico and Arizona*
F. W. Hodge's *The Handbook of North American Indians*
A. M. Smith's *The Indians of New Mexico*
D. S. Matson and A. H. Schroeder's *A Colony on the Move*
D. F. Johnston's *An Analysis of Sources of Information on Population of the Navaho*
Commissioner's Reports of the Bureau of Indian Affairs
Census Reports of the Bureau of Census
Unpublished data in the possession of the Arizona State Museum Library.

The data were carefully examined to determine the original source. In cases of contradictory data for the same year, an average was taken in order to minimize the error caused by a single estimate. These population figures appear in Table 2, while Pueblo Sum (based on sum estimates) appear as Figure 4. However, any data based on the 1870 census were ignored due to its well-known inaccuracy with regard to Indian population, as were data based on Father Benevides, the 17th century custodian of New Mexico missions. Other problems of data accuracy will be discussed in the section of this chapter entitled "Limitations of Data."

Determination of the Contact Variable

The problem of measuring contact in the Pueblos is a complex one. First, the contact has not been simply the bilateral contact through time of a dominant society with a subservient one. During the late 16th and early 17th centuries, it is clear that the Pueblos were the dominant society. The Spanish caused a minor economic drain, but had little influence over Pueblo culture as a whole. By the latter half of the 17th century, the roles had been reversed – the Spanish were dominant, and the Pueblos subservient. This reversal and the resulting oppression stimulated the revolt of 1680. Second, there was a diversity of contacting cultures. The Spaniards, Mexicans, and Anglo-Americans each had assimilation programs based upon their own particular traditions, mores, and cultural values. Although each attempted to change the life patterns of the Pueblos, each was differently motivated and focused upon different institutions. Spicer (1962: 280) characterized each:

The Spaniards, whatever may have been the special concerns of particular governors and missionary orders, inaugurated a program for civilization which was guided most definitely by a religious orientation. Obviously, there were also strong economic interests which influenced high policy and affected the local administration of the program. But, the basic conception of what the Spaniards wanted to accomplish in New Spain was clearly defined as religious conversion, and repeatedly when that purpose was seriously interfered with by local development of economic interests the conflict was resolved in favor of the missionary programs. . . . The emphasis in Mexican policy was on political, rather than religious values. In so far as any organized program of assimilation developed, it was oriented toward the implantation of new political behavior and the integration of Indians as individuals or in communities into the Mexican republican system. The Anglo-American program of assimilation is more difficult to characterize. . . . Nevertheless, it seems fair to define it as a program guided primarily by economic focus.

In addition to the programs for assimilation, there was continued Pueblo contact with other aboriginal populations. As early as 1590, de Sosa reported groups of nomads camped just outside the pueblos. Schroeder and Matson (1965) suggest that these were Apaches or Plains Indians. After the suppression of the revolt of 1680, the period 1694-1710 found the inhabitants of Jémez, as well as other resistant Tanoans and Tewas, fleeing to the mountains, joining the Navajos, or moving to the Hopi mesas. On the other hand, by 1846, Navajo, Ute, Comanche, and Apache war parties were noted for their raids on the Pueblos to supplement their herds and capture slaves

TABLE 2
Adjusted Population Figures for New Mexico Pueblos, 1599-1963

Date	Ácoma	Santa Ana	San Ildefonso	Isleta	Santo Domingo	Taos	Tesuque	Zuñi	Zía
1599	3000								
1620									
1630	2000					2500		10000	
1641			400				170		
1680	1500		800	2000	150	2000	200	2500	
1681				1481					
1712									
1749			354				507		
1760	1052	404	484	304	424	505	232	664	568
1776			387						
1780									
1788				2103	608	578		1617	1035
1790	820	356	240	410	650	518	138	1935	375
1797	757	634	251	603	1453	531	155	2716	262
1798									
1800	800								
1805	731	450	175	419	333	508	131	1470	254
1809	816	550	283		720	527	160		256
1819				487					
1820								1597	
1850	367	339	319	751	666	361	119	1294	124
1860	523	316	166	440	262	363	97	1300	115
1864	491	298		786	604	361	101		163
1871	436	373	156	768	735	397	98		121
1874	500	500	510		1000	375	125	1560	125
1878				1200					
1880								1650	
1889	582	264	189	1037	930	324	94	1547	113
1890	581	262	151	1033	820	401	102		108
1900	492	228	137	1035	771	462	80	1525	115
1902	566								
1904	735	224	154	979	846	465	86	1521	116
1905	739	226	250	989	1000	425	100	1514	125
1910	891	219	114	956	817	517	80	1667	109
1920							109		
1924	955	224	97	1003	1054	622	111	1949	154
1940									
1950	1376	285	152	1051	978	842	145	2564	145
1963	1674	336	224	1974	1495	896	142	4704	377

Nambé	Pojoaque	Picurís	Laguna	Cochití	Sandía	Jémez	San Juan	San Felipe	Santa Clara
		2000							
						3000			
300									
600		3000		300	3000	5000	300	600	300
	79								
							404		
264	99	326	600	450	291	373	316	458	257
	98	223					201		
		212	1368		596				452
155	53	254	668	720	304	485	260	532	134
178	79	251	802	505	116	272	202	282	193
	79								
143	100	250	940	656	314	264	194	289	186
133		313	1022	697	364	297	208	405	220
107	48	222	749	254	241	365	568	800	279
107	37	143	929	172	217	650	343	360	179
94	29	122	988	229	197	342	385	427	144
78	32	127	927	243	186	344	426	482	189
160	20	150	900	400	225	800	350	400	50
		120	970	300	150	474	373		187
80	18								
86		91	1063	277	143	455	390	527	204
81	12	95	1077	247	81	452	422	515	222
100		101	1366	217	79	489	419	489	251
100		125	1384	300	74	450	425	475	
88	16	104	1472	237	73	449	388	502	243
							290		
128		105	1901	267	92	580	458	526	339
	23								
96	2	99	1655	289	150	789	152	721	511
135	41	100	2956	387	124	1076	670	1060	535

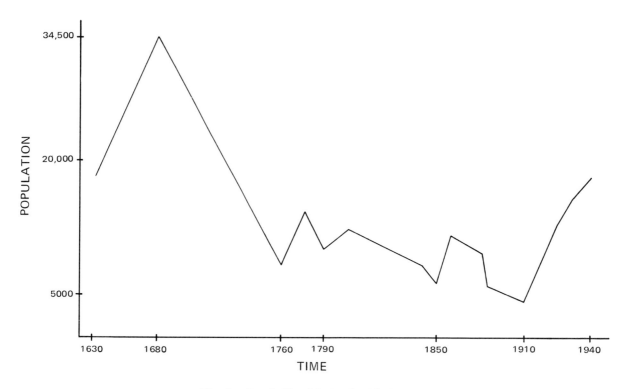

Fig. 4.　Total: New Mexico Pueblo Population.

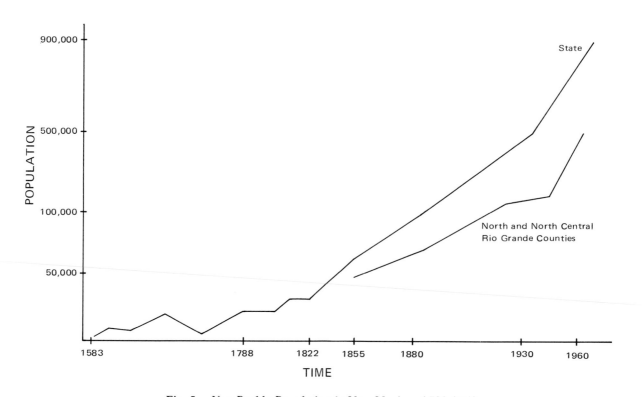

Fig. 5.　Non-Pueblo Population in New Mexico: 1583-1960.

(Johnston 1966). Later Anglo boarding school policy brought contact with Plains Indians and more distant tribes (La Farge 1959).

Considering the variation in (1) dominance and subservience, (2) the contacting cultures and their motivations, and (3) the focus of the contact, as well as the differences in Pueblo cultures, it is not surprising that the resulting acculturation and diffusion are neither homogeneous nor evenly distributed among Pueblo institutions, and are therefore difficult to quantify. In order to develop an index of contact, I have made the assumption that cultural contact is a function of the amount of population contact. By population contact I mean, in the Brownian Motion sense, the interrelationships which must develop as individuals or groups of individuals move within a limited area. The actual size of the area is partially determined by ecological, territorial, and proxemic variables. The greater the number of individuals or the restriction of the area, however, the greater the probability that there will be some form of intercommunication between various individuals or groups. It may take one of several forms, such as warfare, trade, extensions of kin ties, slavery, or religious communication. One may postulate with reasonable confidence that a culture faced with a continually increasing number of non-members in its environment must adapt to this change through some mechanism. A culture cannot ignore this increase in "foreigners" completely — especially in the case of the Pueblos, where there was an increase in non-native population of approximately 500 to 500,000 in a 350-year period. At the very least, an increase in non-members places a strain on limited resources.

In order to determine the amount of population contact, I have utilized the term *non-native population,* which does not mean non-Indian population. *Non-native population* is defined as total population minus Pueblo Sum, and is presented in Figure 5.

Limitations of the Data

First one must examine native population data. Since population contact equals total population minus native population, the inaccuracies in native population data are reflected in population contact. In general the defects of all population data — lack of completeness, simultaneity, standardization, and definition — apply to both contact and native. The early data are based on estimates of Spanish travelers, colonists, and missionaries. There is no way of determining their accuracy other than by reasonable comparison and extrapolation from present-day figures. One solution to this problem might be an analysis of the number of rooms per pueblo during each time period, in conjunction with the Turner-Lafgren estimation figures. As will be seen later, however, this methodology does not provide the actual variation, but averages the various villages.

Two patterns of inaccuracy appear in the early data. First, during periods of hostility, there is a tendency to overestimate the population of the Pueblos as enemies, particularly in their counts of potential able-bodied warriors. Second, there is a tendency for the missionaries to exaggerate the number of Indians they have successfully converted.

The Bureau of Indian Affairs, with its original functions of treaties and trade, was organized in 1824 as part of the War Department. With its transfer to the Department of the Interior in 1849, the Bureau's custodial function became manifest. Some of the agents began including demographic data as part of their reports to the commissioner. The agents varied with regard to their thoroughness and familiarity with the population under their administration. Certain agents sent detailed demographic reports to help substantiate their requests for economic aid, while others did not bother to state more than the fact that they and their charges were still alive. Once more we are limited to the probity value of each agent.

The later, more sophisticated Bureau of Indian Affairs and Bureau of Census reports have been faced with a series of definitional and operational problems. First, should the Pueblos be considered at the community or tribal level of analysis? Second, what is a Pueblo Indian? Is the designation determined by genetic, geographic, or cultural criteria? The Bureau of Census has defined the American Indian, for what appears to be historical reasons, by blood relationship. The present definition is:

In addition to full blooded American Indians, persons of mixed white and Indian blood are included in this category if they are enrolled on an Indian tribal or agency role or if they are regarded as Indians in their community. A common requirement for such enrollment at present is that the proportion of Indian blood should be at least one-fourth. [Bureau of Census 1963: X]

Prior to 1960, in addition to the above, the following was added:

The information on race is ordinarily not based on a reply to questions asked by the enumerator but rather is obtained by observation (Bureau of Census 1953: 4).

The skewing of data inherent in the use of the above definition is increased by the variations in coverage and accuracy of the individual census takers. Furthermore, extensive information on tribal affiliation was gathered only in 1890, 1910, and 1930. Thus, during the 1940s and 1950s some of the data (particularly that published by Indian Agencies) were the extrapolations of county proportions.

In order to arrive at an independent estimate of the population of each pueblo, I utilized 1950 aerial photographs and ground maps of 17 of the 18 pueblos (Pojoaque was not available) (Stubbs 1950). After calculating the total number of rooms per pueblo, I divided the population by the number of rooms. The range was from .764 to 10.728 people per room, as compared with the estimates of Turner and Lafgren (1966) of 5.134 for A.D. 1300-1600 and 7.015 for A.D. 1600-1900. The variation is being averaged in the Turner-Lafgren method. Table 3 consists of multiplying the Turner-Lafgren estimates by the number of rooms per pueblo, and thus represents an independent estimate of population.

In addition to the several problems noted for the population contact variable as related to the "native" population, there must be delineated a major problem more uniquely associated with the contact variable. Although the pueblos have reasonably clear geographic boundaries, there are difficulties in locating spatially the contact population. The early Spanish estimates were based on an area consisting of present-day Arizona, New Mexico, and parts of Northern Mexico. It was not until 1863 that Arizona as a Territory was separated from New Mexico. Although county and tract boundaries changed, it is possible to isolate after 1850 meaningful population figures for the counties in which the pueblos occur (see the lower graph in Fig. 5).

Before leaving the population variables, one should note two positive factors. First, the population data of Table 2 are based on contemporary estimates and censuses. Since these data are not based upon settlement pattern assumptions, they are the preferred type of the two types of population data available for the pueblos over the 376-year time span. In spite of limitations, the data are the best available. Second, as will be shown in the next chapter, it is possible through non-parametric statistical analysis to minimize the inaccuracies in the data.

TABLE 3
Population Estimates for 1950, Based on Turner-Lafgren Index

Pueblo	Number of Rooms (Stubbs 1950)	Population Estimates (Number of Rooms x the Turner-Lafgren Index)
San Ildefonso	199	1396
Laguna	187	1312
Sandía	79	554
San Felipe	273	1915
Isleta	627	4398
Santo Domingo	413	2897
San Juan	174	1221
Nambé	33	231
Picurís	54	379
Santa Ana	133	932
Zía	121	849
Ácoma	361	2532
Jémez	397	2785
Taos	526	3690
Santa Clara	142	996
Cochití	140	982
Tesuque	101	709
Zuñi	239	1677

Similar to the population variables, the climatic variable has limitations which must be examined, and errors which must be compensated for if possible. Foremost among these limitations is the utilizing of a single, refined, climatological index to describe partially variable climatic conditions over a considerable area. Maxon (1966: 3,4,10) concludes, after a thorough analysis of present-day climatic conditions relating to snow, precipitation, frost, and temperature data that:

While the area is generally semi-arid, climate conditions vary mainly with altitude, which varies several thousand feet from north to south. The northern area around Taos is higher and generally more moist and cool than Albuquerque to the south. . . . Fairly long, relatively dry winters are experienced in the north with below zero temperatures possible from November through February. Annual snowfall varies from about 30 inches or more at elevations of 7000 feet or above, down to less than 10 inches in the Albuquerque area. Temperatures rarely reach zero in the Albuquerque area, but they may reach 90-100 degrees from May through September.

TABLE 4
Comparison of Ethnohistorical and Dendrochronological Climatic Data*

Date	Ethnohistorical Statement	Reference	Fritts' Relative Departure	Agreement
1540	Coronado encountered heavy snow and intense cold at Tiguex: the Rio Grande was frozen.	Bancroft 1962: 59	.31 .31	+
1541	Rio Grande was frozen until May; rainy season became a hindrance to transportation in Sept. and Oct.	Bancroft 1962: 59	.31 −.37	−
1591	Santo Domingo which was then located at Galisteo Arroyo was flooded; De Sosa encountered heavy snow and pine forest near Santo Domingo and San Felipe.	White 1935: 12	−.06 .37	+
1638	Father Juan de Prada in a petition describes missions of New Mexico as having rigorous winters with excessive cold and snow — the rivers freeze over; but the summers are hot.	Hackett 1937: 109	.72 .05	+
1639	Francisco Martínez de Baeza in a petition describes a severe winter similar to the ones mentioned above.	Hackett 1937: 119-20	.72 .05	+
1640	General drought mentioned by Vivian in which 3000 Indians die of starvation, presumably documented in Spanish archival materials (no reference).	Vivian 1964: 153	.72 .05	−
1663-1669	Province-wide drought causes abandonment of Gran Quivira; 1668 saw 450 Indians die of starvation.	Vivian 1964: 153	.23 −.34 −.42	+
1670	Crop failure in half the province.	Hackett 1937: 17	−.42 .12	+
1706	Father Fray Juan Álvarez at Nambé on January 12 reports the road from Santa Fe to Pecos closed in times of heavy snow, and ice on the Rio Grande near San Ildefonso and Santo Domingo.	Hackett 1937: 375	−.03 .23	+
1744	Fray Miguel de Menchero notes crystalline river full of trout flowing through Santa Fe; today river totally dry during summer and intermittent during rest of year.	Hackett 1937: 27, 34, 399	−.22 −.20	−
1760	Bishop Tamarón describes Santa Fe river as dry several months before harvest, however, winters cold with ice on Rio Grande and the fruit trees at Isleta didn't bear fruit. Below Albuquerque areas flooded and needed a canoe to cross Rio Grande at Cochití.	Adams 1954: 47, 65 105	−.31 −.05	+ −
1774	Province-wide drought (source not clear).	Kidder 1958: 312	.32 −.23	−
1776	There is a drought and irrigation is necessary at all pueblos — reported by Fray Francisco Domínguez.	Adams and Chavez 1956: 112, 217	−.23 −.15	+

*Abstracted from Maxon and Fritts

TABLE 4 Continued

Date	Ethnohistorical Statement	Reference	Fritts' Relative Departure	Agreement
1780	Father Marfi states that pastures were sparse when snows light which indicates little summer rain.	White 1935: 16-19	-.23 -.15	+
1782	Father Marfi reports flooding of the Rio Grande destroys Santa Ana farming.	White 1942: 27-8	-.15 -.24	-
1832	Antonio Barreiro describes the climate as being colder than Europe at the same latitude; he notes the rivers are frozen enough to support mounted men and pack trains.	Carroll and Haggard 1942	.80 .85	+
Mid-1850s	Davis claims that agriculture was hampered by lack of regular and frequent rain.	Davis 1857: 195	-.43 -.38 .10 -.39	+
1868	Pueblo Indian agent reports flood damage.	Bancroft 1962: 739-40	-.28 .33	+
1873	Pueblo Indian agent reports crop failure.	Bancroft 1962: 739-40	.33 -.20	-
1874	Pueblo Indian agent reports good crops.	Bancroft 1962: 739-40	.33 -.20	+
1877	Pueblo Indian agent reports poor crops.	Bancroft 1962: 739-40	-.20 -.04	+
1886	Santo Domingo was hit by a severe flood which destroyed a large portion of the pueblo.	White 1935: 12	.39 .10	+
1890	Special agent Porre mentions more flooding at Santo Domingo and that Indians would not plant in river bottom for fear of flooding by the Rio Grande.	White 1935: 20-21	.39 .10	+
1896	Taos, found water scarce in July and depended upon irrigation although it was usually described as being in a well-watered valley.	Miller 1898: 22	.10 -.29	+

Elevations of 7000 feet or above are found in the Rio Grande Valley itself in the Taos area, and in the highlands bordering the Rio Grande basin from about La Bajada Hill about 40 miles north of Albuquerque northward to Taos. . . .

The period of June through August receives the most precipitation. This moisture does come when it is most useful for growing crops, but with yearly totals of only 8.1 to 14.27 inches, it is evident that irrigation would normally be necessary for dependable year to year farming. Also summer rains are occasionally so severe as to do more harm than good through farming.

The non-parametric correlation technique used in the next chapter partially adjusts the data by ignoring minor differentiations and concentrating on major trends.

A second problem, which has consequences far less serious, is that Fritts' data are presented in ten-year averages staggered at five-year intervals, for example, 1711-20, 1716-25, and 1721-30. The population data are specific to a given year and do not always fall on the mean date of the periods. However, when resolution of this problem becomes essential, as in the correlation, compensation has been achieved by utilizing the parametric nature of the data to calculate the weighted mean which falls upon the date in question.

As previously mentioned, Fritts based the validity of his 270-year standard interval and index on a close correspondence and accurate prediction of climatic conditions of the last 50 years, checked against Weather Bureau reports. In order to obtain an independent test of the data, it is possible to examine the climatic references of ethnohistorical and archaeological sources, and compare them to Fritts' data. Maxon (1966) has analyzed data, culling out the climatic references which he compared to Fritts' major conclusions. In Table 4 I have abstracted Maxon's data and compared them to Fritts' actual non-adjusted data; it is clear that there is a high degree of correspondence.

Of the 24 climatic references in this table, 17 agreed with Fritts, 6 disagreed, and 1 agreed or disagreed depending upon the part of the description considered — or 71 percent, 25 percent, and 4 percent respectively. Ignoring the one reference with two interpretations, $\chi^2 = 5.262$, which has a less than 5 percent probability of being caused by chance. This is well within the usual criteria for scientific use. One is justified, therefore, in stating that the ethnohistorical and archaeological references — the independent test — substantiate Fritts' data.

CHAPTER 3

POPULATION VARIATION, POPULATION-CLIMATE CORRELATION, RESULTS, AND CONCLUSIONS OF THE FIRST TEST

Degree of Population Variation

If one plots the pueblo population data through time, a clear series of patterned variation is apparent. For example, Ácoma, Taos, and Zuñi follow a "U" shape pattern. That is, the population first decreases and then increases through time: Tesuque, Zía, Nambé, Picurís, Jémez, and Pueblo Sum have a ⋏ shape; Isleta and San Felipe a "W" shape. The other pueblos may also be classified into groups. The results of this plotting analysis would be sufficient to tentatively indicate different processes at work in the various groups of pueblos.

One of the more accurate ways of determining population variation is to discover the equation that best describes each group of data and compare all of these equations. This has been done for each pueblo and for Pueblo Sum. The equations were defined by utilizing the BMD 05R Polynomial Regression program of the Biomedical Computer Programs published by the University of California Press. This analysis showed: (1) what was true in terms of population size for the pueblos as a group, was not necessarily true for each pueblo individually; (2) at least five different order equations were necessary to describe adequately (99 percent probability of not occurring by chance) the variation in population changes from pueblo to pueblo.

This program computes polynomial regressions of the form:

$$Y = \alpha + B_1 X + B_2 X^2 + \cdots + B_k X^k + e$$

where k is some positive integer.

Letting $Z_{ij} = X_1^j$ $i = 1, 2, \cdots n$ $j = 1, 2, \cdots k$

The sums of the products are computed after the means have been subtracted from Z_{ij} and Y_i.

$$A = \sum_{k=1}^{n} (Z_{ki} - \bar{Z}_i)(Z_{kj} - \bar{Z}_j)$$

$$t = \sum_{k=1}^{n} (Z_{ki} - \bar{Z}_i)(Y_k - \bar{Y})$$

$$S = \sum_{k=1}^{n} (Y_k - \bar{Y})^2$$

For each $m = 1, 2, \ldots k$ the following were computed and printed:

Regression coefficients $B = A^{-1} t$

Y intercepts $\bar{Y} - \sum_{i=1}^{m} B_i \bar{Z}_i$

Sum of the Squares for Regression $R = t'B$
Error Sum of the Squares $E = S - R$
F Statistic $(n - m - 1) \dfrac{R/m}{E}$
Standard Error $B_i = \sqrt{Ea^{ii}/(n - m - 1)}$

A table of residuals was produced for the final degree of polynomial regression, and a plot was made of the observed and predicted values from the regression equation. K was limited to no more than 10 by the library program; in other words, we delineated the equations of tenth degree or smaller which best fitted the data. These results were statistically significant for all 20 groups of data.

TABLE 5
Results of the Regression Analysis Using F Test

| | Degree Equations | | | | | | | | | | |
Pueblo	First 95 99		Second 95 99		Third 95 99		Fourth 95 99		Fifth 95 99		Sixth 95 99	
Santa Clara	–	–	+	+	+	+	+	+	+	+	+	+
Pueblo Sum	+	+	+	+	+	+	+	+	+	+	+	+
Ácoma	+	+	+	+	+	+	+	+	+	+	+	+
Santa Ana	+	+	+	–	+	+	+	+	+	+	+	–
San Ildefonso	+	+	+	+	+	+	+	+	+	+	+	+
Isleta	–	–	+	+	+	–	+	–	–	–	+	–
Santo Domingo	+	+	+	–	+	–	+	–	–	–	+	–
Taos	+	+	+	+	+	+	+	+	+	+	+	+
Tesuque	+	–	+	–	+	+	+	+	+	+	+	+
Zuñi	+	–	+	+	+	+	+	+	+	+	+	+
Zía	+	–	+	+	+	+	+	–	+	+	+	–
Nambé	+	+	+	+	+	+	+	+	+	+	+	+
Pojoaque	+	+	+	+	+	+	+	+	+	+	+	+
Picurís	+	+	+	+	+	+	+	+	+	+	+	+
Laguna	+	+	+	+	+	+	+	+	+	+	+	+
Cochití	+	–	–	–	+	+	+	+	+	+	+	+
Sandía	+	+	+	+	+	+	+	+	+	+	+	+
Jémez	+	+	+	+	+	+	+	+	+	+	+	+
San Juan	+	–	–	–	–	–	–	–	+	+	+	–
San Felipe	–	–	+	+	+	+	+	+	+	+	+	+

Does the Population Correlate With Climate?

In order to determine the relationships between population and climate, I utilized Kendall's non-parametric coefficient of concordance. It is necessary to briefly explain why the non-parametric test was utilized rather than a parametric correlation coefficient such as the Pearson Product Moment coefficient. Parametric coefficients are based upon the assumption that the samples have been drawn from a normal population. In some cases, this assumption looks quite unreasonable. Non-parametric or distribution-free methods allow one to make inferences without any assumption as to the form of the distribution in the population. In the case of our "population" variables where the data are not based upon a representative sampling procedure but on available data, we have no concrete basis for making the normality assumption.

A second reason for utilizing the non-parametric route is the lack of refined precision in our data. By calculating a rank order coefficient, one correlates the relative positions in a series of ranks rather than the actual data. If the data were 16, 5, 7, 11, they would be ranked 4, 1, 2, 3. In a parametric test, if the first number were 15 rather than 16, there would be a different value for the correlation coefficient. In a non-parametric rank test, however, this variation would make no difference since 15 would still be ranked 4. For the population data, based upon estimates and averages, it is clear that the relative positions of the data as ranks are more likely to be correct than the actual values of the data.

I utilized Kendall's concordance rather than the more common Kendall's or Spearman's rho, since it allows for the possibility of correlating two or more variables. It is defined in the following manner:

$$\text{If} \qquad U = \sum_{i=1}^{N} R_1 \cdots R_N$$

$$V = (\sum_{i=1}^{n} R_1 \cdots R_N)^2$$

Then

$$S = V - U^2/N \quad W = \frac{12S}{M^2 \, N(N^2-1)}$$

The F test is related to W by

$$F = \frac{(M-1)\,W}{1-W}$$

Where the n limits for the F significance test is:

$$n_1 = N - 1 - 2/M$$

$$n_2 = (M-1)(N-1-2/M)$$

Where:

U	=	the sum of the ranks for the variables R_1 through R_n
V	=	the sum of the ranks squared
W	=	the coefficient of concordance
F	=	the F test
n_1	=	the numerator degrees of freedom
n_2	=	the denominator degrees of freedom
M	=	the number of variables
N	=	the number of members within a variable

If N and M were small, the correction for continuity was made by subtracting 1 from S and increasing the divisor of W by 2 so that:

$$W' = \frac{12S\,(S-1)}{m^2 N\,(N^2-1)+24} \quad \text{and} \quad F = \frac{3W'}{1-W'}$$

In order to determine if there were temporal differentiation in the relationship between climate and native population, I divided the time span into two periods. The period prior to and including 1800 was compared with the period from 1801 to the present. The results of this analysis may be seen in Table 6.

Discussion of the Results

The results of this analysis of raw data and the application of various statistical tests are summarized in Figures 4 and 5, Tables 5 and 6. First, it is clear that the population contact variable (non-Rio Grande and non-Zuñi Pueblo population), is continually increasing over time (Fig. 5). Second, if we compare climate to population for the Rio Grande Pueblos as a group prior to 1800, there is no relationship between the two variables. However, after 1800, there is a

relationship. Turning to Table 6, Pueblo Sum is correlated with climate at the 95 percent level of significance after 1800; this direct relationship cannot be explained by chance. Prior to 1800, the correlation is not statistically significant.

Third, one might be tempted to assume that what affects the group also affects the individual members. However, noting the population plots and regression analysis, this mistake would be dangerous. There may be considerably different types of population changes taking place; therefore, one must look at each pueblo separately.

Fourth, examining each pueblo separately, one notes in Table 6 that only Santo Domingo correlates population with climate before 1800, while after 1800, Taos, Zuñi, and Santo Domingo correlate at least at a 95 percent level of significance.

Conclusions of the First Test

A simple examination of the population contact variable eliminates the possibility of hypotheses 5-8 being valid. The fact that the correlation of Pueblo Sum with climate improves over time (invalid pre-1800, valid post-1800) forces the rejection of hypothesis 2, the primary hypothesis, and hypothesis 4. Hypothesis 1 must be rejected since the primary population increase is in the late seventeenth and early eighteenth century, where there is no valid correlation between climate and population. The data support hypothesis 3, which states that as population contact increases and native population decreases, the importance of the climatic variable increases.

Before turning to a more detailed analysis, I will quickly summarize an alternative explanation for the data's corroboration of hypothesis 3. When viewed within the context of the other evidence, this hypothesis is not as strange as it first appears. Although the hypothesis applies to the pueblos as a group, it does not apply to them individually. In fact, for 14 pueblos, there are no correlations between climate and population.

The pueblo area as a whole has only a limited carrying capacity (a limited number of people it can feed through a given technology), as does each area surrounding an individual pueblo. The sum of the individual carrying capacities equals the total carrying capacity for the entire area. When faced with increasing population contact, there is a greater strain upon the carrying capacity of each individual pueblo and

TABLE 6
Correlation of Population With Climate

Pueblo	Time Period	W	F	Level of Significance 95%	99%
Pueblo Sum	post-1800	.74285	2.8888	+	–
Taos	post-1800	.73131	2.7218	+	–
Zuñi	post-1800	.83787	5.1679	+	+
Santo Domingo	post-1800	.74420	2.9090	+	–
Santo Domingo	pre-1800	.96250	25.6666	+	–
Pueblo Sum	pre-1800	.50714	1.0289	–	–
Zuñi	pre-1800	.69285	2.2557	–	–
Taos	pre-1800	.33250	.49812	–	–
Isleta	pre-1800	.39285	.64700	–	–
Isleta	post-1800	.68351	2.1596	–	–
Ácoma	pre-1800	.57142	1.3333	–	–
Ácoma	post-1800	.68314	2.1586	–	–
San Juan	pre-1800	.42857	.75000	–	–
San Juan	post-1800	.57232	1.3381	–	–
Laguna	pre-1800	.77500	3.4444	–	–
Laguna	post-1800	.68901	2.2155	–	–
Zía	pre-1800	.17500	.21212	–	–
Zía	post-1800	.36852	.58360	–	–
Cochití	pre-1800	.90000	9.0000	–	–
Cochití	post-1800	.50714	1.0289	–	–
Nambé	pre-1800	.10000	.11111	–	–
Nambé	post-1800	.32472	.47990	–	–
San Ildefonso	pre-1800	.16071	.19148	–	–
San Ildefonso	post-1800	.31730	.46477	–	–
Pojoaque	pre-1800	.24042	.31652	–	–
Pojoaque	post-1800	.35833	.55843	–	–
Picurís	pre-1800	.37944	.61150	–	–
Picurís	post-1800	.35494	.55024	–	–
Santa Clara	pre-1800	.28750	.40350	–	–
Santa Clara	post-1800	.66878	2.0282	–	–
San Felipe	pre-1800	.10000	.11111	–	–
San Felipe	post-1800	.66140	1.9533	–	–
Sandía	pre-1800	.16250	.19402	–	–
Sandía	post-1800	.30000	.42857	–	–
Jémez	pre-1800	.35000	.53850	–	–
Jémez	post-1800	.53747	1.1163	–	–
Santa Ana	pre-1800	.75000	3.0000	–	–
Santa Ana	post-1800	.33296	.49920	–	–
Tesuque	pre-1800	.10000	.11111	–	–
Tesuque	post-1800	.33401	.50152	–	–

pre-1800 (inclusive)
post-1800 (exclusive)

upon the resources of the entire area (i.e., competition for limited resources increases). Climatic variation has a minor effect on carrying capacity, which continues to be minor in the disequilibrium situation as long as the population contact and the consequent deprivation of resources are below the critical threshold. This condition appears to have existed prior to 1800, since there is no relationship between Pueblo Sum and climate. However, after 1800, when the strain on limited resources becomes acute, the variation of climate becomes a significant determinant of native population, as can be seen by the correlation of Pueblo Sum and climate. The differentiated results between the area as a unit and the individual pueblo as a unit might be explained by an economic trade network. This network, either native-supported or BIA-supported, was partially able to offset the deprivation resulting from intense competition for limited resources which existed in any individual pueblo, but not in the entire area.

Consider the Rio Grande Pueblos as individual economic and ecological units. The ecological differences are obvious from the aerial photographs (Figures 6-24): differing location of fields, proximity to water, and amount and type of land cover. As economic units, there are differing amounts of food and goods per capita for each pueblo. In order to demonstrate this variability, I have calculated the population per utilized agricultural acre as an index for each pueblo. These indices, which appear in Table 7, are based upon raw data presented in the special report of the 1893 census and the Memoir Number 70 of the *American Anthropologist* (Aberle: 1948). The range in 1890 was from .161 to 1.080, and in 1944, from .074 to 4.689. These ranges reflect the differences in productivity and the importance of agriculture for the pueblos, and there is considerable variation.

In comparison to the above, it is possible to consider the pueblos as one macro-economic and ecological unit. Ecologically there are many similarities. For climate, one needs only note the climatic unity as presented in Chapter 2. Each pueblo's lands consist of a tripartite division—utilizable agricultural lands, grazing lands, and semi-arid waste lands. (In the case of Taos, the semi-arid waste lands are replaced by mountains.) The agricultural lands have been developed by a changing mixture of flood, irrigation, and dry farming. The grazing lands differ from the arid waste lands in the amount of succulence in what

TABLE 7
Index of Economic Variability
in 1890 and 1944*

Pueblo	1890	1944
Ácoma	+**	.950
Cochití	+**	.549
Isleta	.397	.376
Jémez	+**	.570
Laguna	+**	.169
Nambé	.286	.500
Picurís	.161	.653
Pojoaque	+**	.714
Sandía	+**	.074
San Felipe	+**	.491
San Ildefonso	+**	.536
San Juan	.609	.781
Santa Ana	.349	.466
Santa Clara	.582	.965
Santo Domingo	+**	.619
Zía or Sía	1.080	.099
Taos	+**	4.689
Tesuque	.443	.471
Zuñi	+**	.818

*Index = population divided by utilized agricultural land.
** – no information available.

botanists usually term the "succulent desert." Economically, not only is there a high degree of similarity in the operation and components of the subsistence agricultural base, there is also a considerable degree of economic solidarity.

Although markets did not develop until comparatively recently — and then under western stimulation — this economic solidarity was manifested in two ways. First, there was a crisis trade mechanism which could be relied upon to trade enough subsistence goods to carry a pueblo population over a short drought or after a major flooding.

The aboriginal pattern was an economy primarily of subsistence. It was useless to raise more corn than your family could consume or store for future use, because there was no market for it. You shared with your neighbor when he was hungry, and he in turn helped you when you needed food. Without money, security lay in a system of social obligation (Aberle 1948: 17).

Fig. 6 Santa Ana Environs and Residential Area

Fig. 7. Ácoma Environs and Residential Area

Fig. 8. Cochití Environs and Residential Area

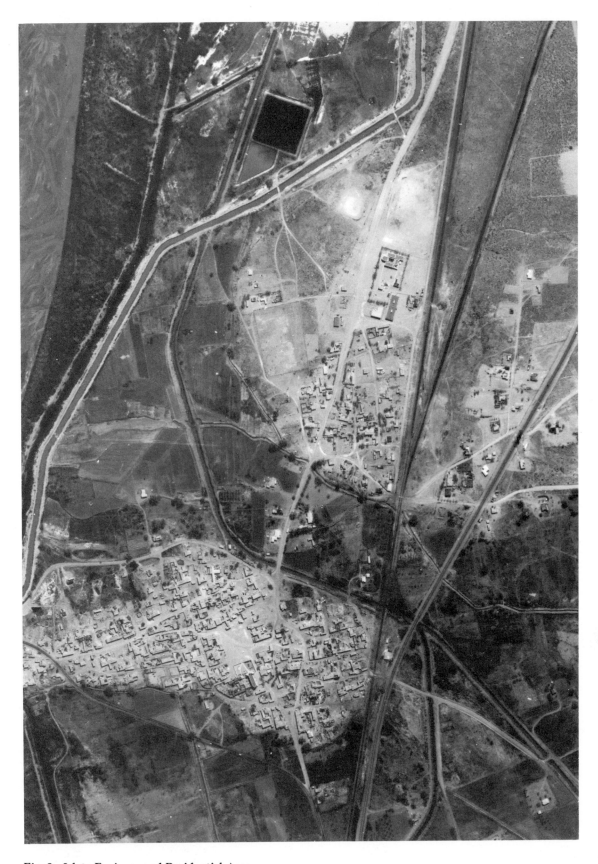

Fig. 9. Isleta Environs and Residential Area

Fig. 10. Jémez Environs and Residential Area

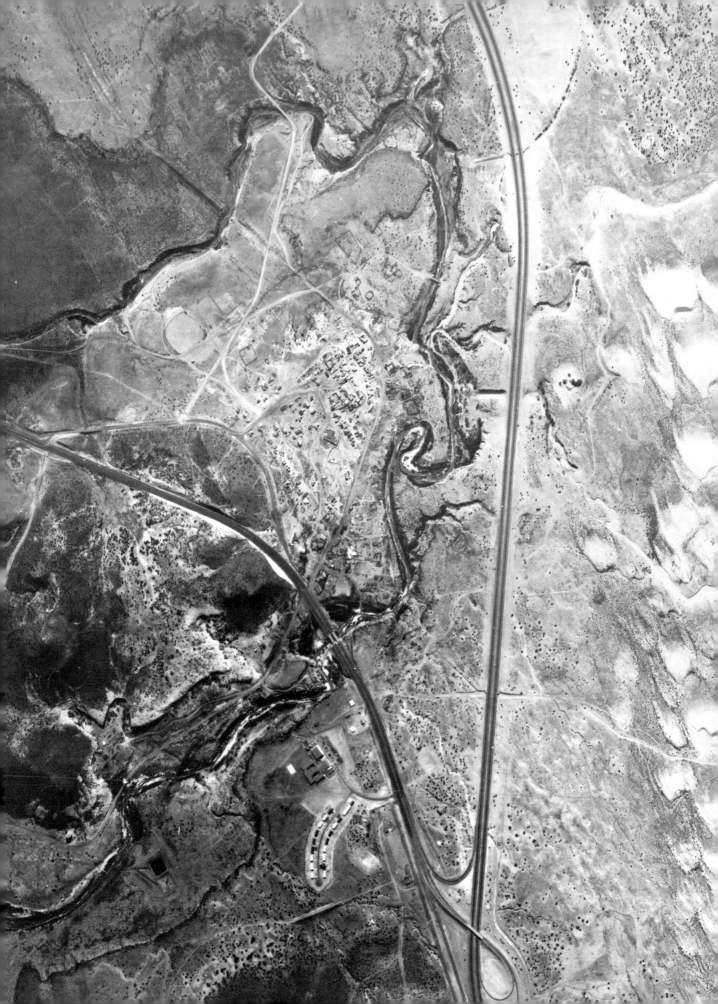

Fig. 11. Laguna Environs and Residential Area

Fig. 12. Nambé Environs and Residential Area

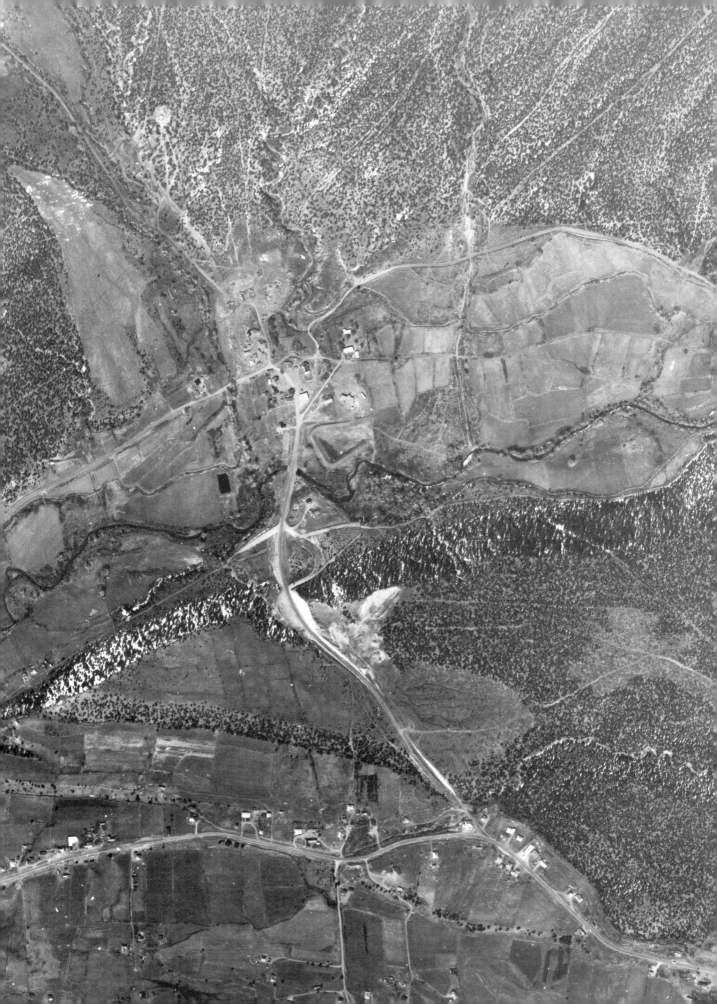

Fig. 13. Picurís Environs and Residential Area

Fig. 14. Pojoaque Environs and Residential Area

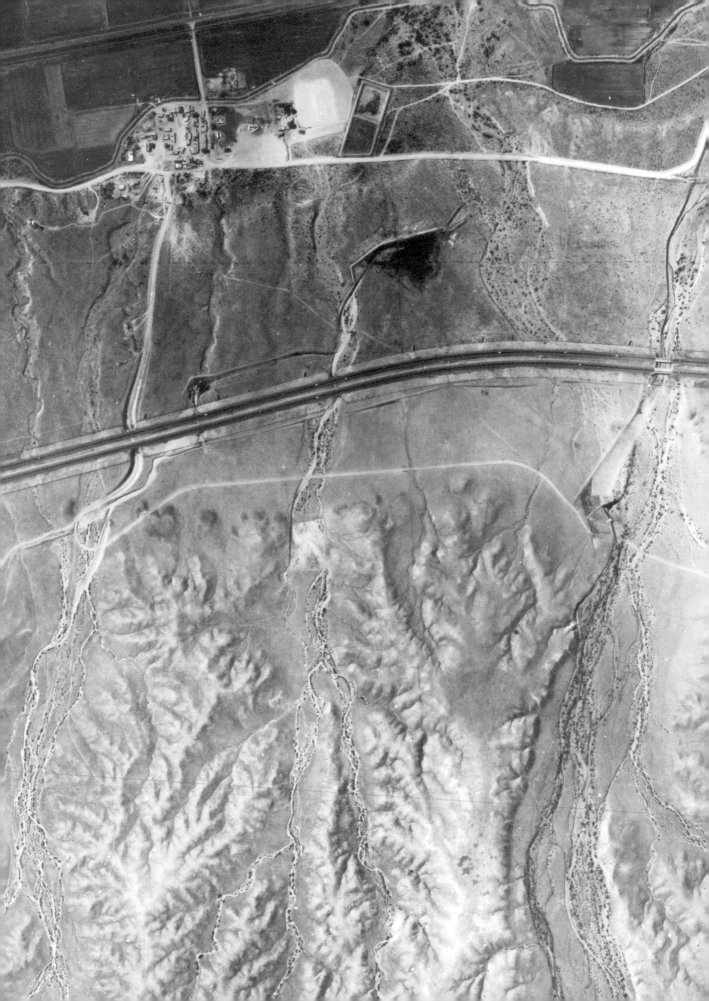

Fig. 15. Sandía Environs and Residential Area

Fig. 16. San Felipe Environs and Residential Area

Fig. 17. San Ildefonso Environs and Residential Area

Fig. 18. San Juan Environs and Residential Area

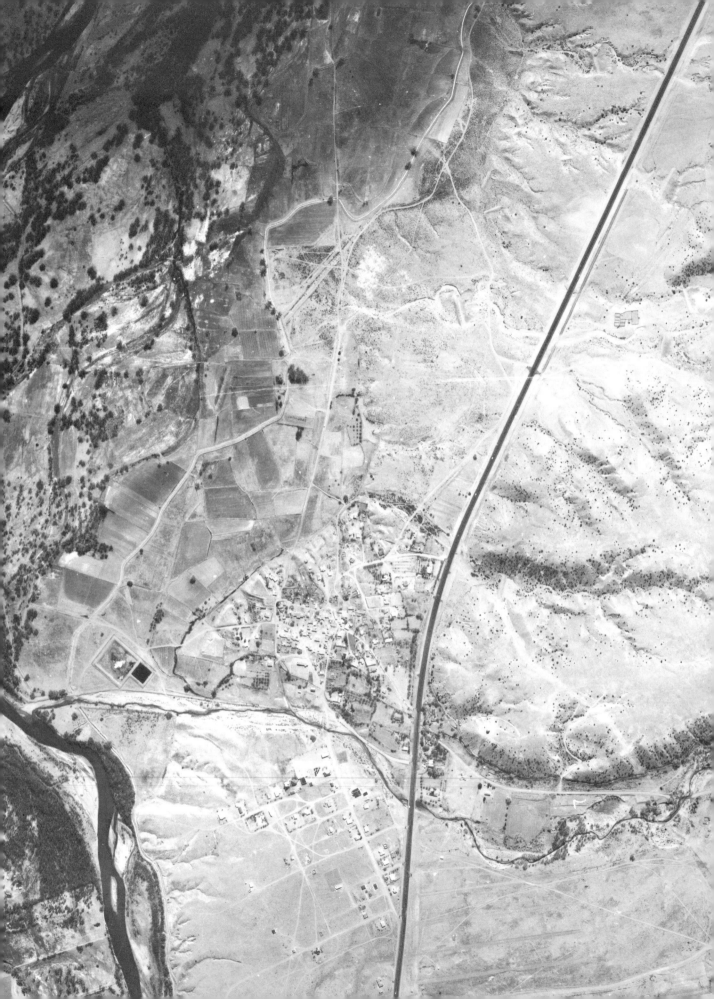

Fig. 19. Santa Clara Environs and Residential Area

Fig. 20. Santo Domingo Environs and Residential Area

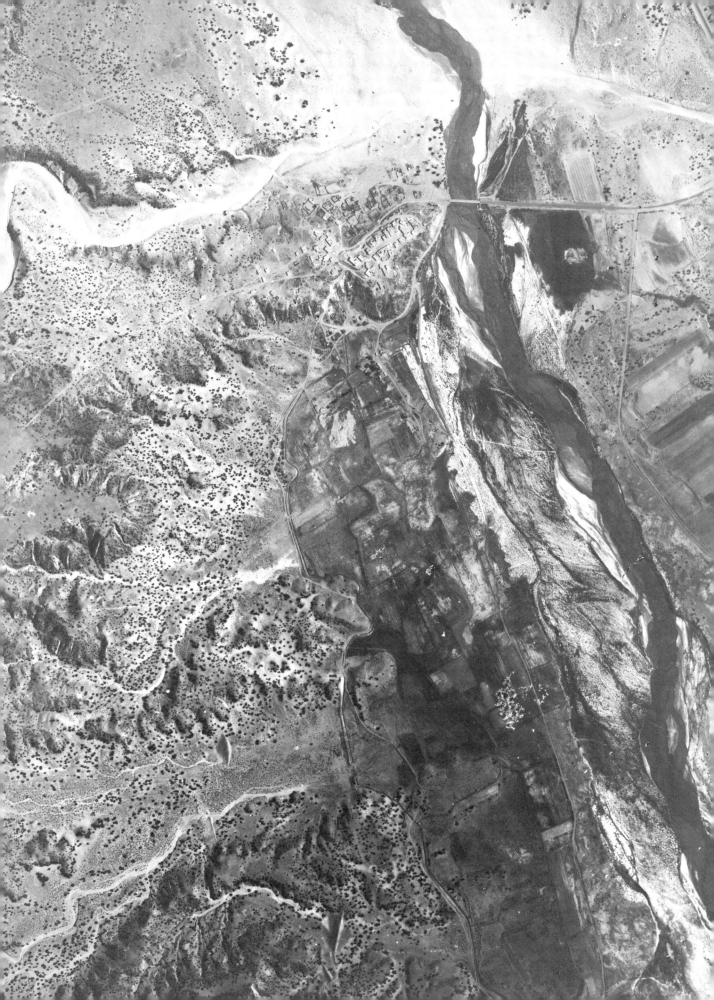

Fig. 21. Zía Environs and Residential Area

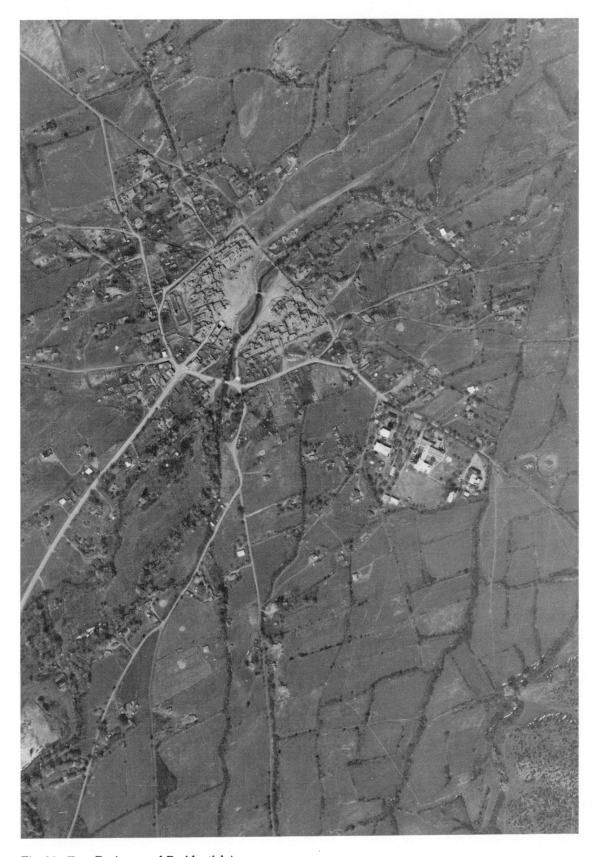

Fig. 22. Taos Environs and Residential Area

Fig. 23. Tesuque Environs and Residential Area

Fig. 24. Zuñi Environs and Residential Area

However, trade between pueblos, if not a continuous process, continued in the long term as an intermittent occupation. Bandelier (1890: 86) claimed:

It may be said that no two tribes were ever so hostile as never to trade, or so intimately connected in friendship as never to fight.

The results of this intermittent trading may be seen in this brief description from Jémez.

There are itinerant traders from other pueblos and Jémez merchants themselves go on trading trips to the other Pueblos and to the Navaho and Jicarilla Apache. . . . In general grapes and chile, melons, wheat and corn are bartered for turquoise, silver belts or necklaces, dress cloth and blankets, buckskin, meat, feathers, and pottery. The women's dresses of native cloth are got from the Hopi and from Santo Domingo, pottery from Santo Domingo and Sía, turquoise from Santo Domingo, blankets and mutton from the Navaho (Parsons 1925: 16).

The second mechanism was short- and long-term migration from a pueblo in a crisis situation (brought on by drought, flooding, or war) to a more prosperous or safely situated pueblo. For example,

Early in June (1696) some of the Tewa and the Indians of Taos, Picurís, Santo Domingo, and Cochití and the resettled Tano of San Cristobal rose in revolt. Twenty-one Spaniards and six priests were killed including Father Francisco Joseph de Arvisu, the resident priest at San Cristobal. After this revolt the Tano of San Cristobal fled west to Zuñi and from there to the Hopi country (Dozier 1954: 273-74).

Another example is the total abandonment of Pecos in 1830, and the absorption of that population into Jémez.

No matter which frame of reference is utilized, there exists a connection between the ecological and the subsistence bases. The limiting factors of the ecology affect the subsistence, although mitigated by culture. There are temperature, water, and length of growing season limitations on all the crops grown by the Pueblos. For example, in an article entitled "Corn Production in New Mexico," J. C. Overpeck (1928: 15) of the Agricultural Experimental Station concludes:

The varied conditions of climate and altitude throughout the state make necessary the growing of quite different varieties. . .

and gives detailed county-by-county planting date information in order to minimize frost problems and maximize growing season.

Furthermore, there is a relationship between climate and irrigation. Most pueblo irrigation is dependent upon streamflow, and it is considered axiomatic that there is a correlation between rainfall and streamflow.

Variation in streamflow depends mainly on geographical and seasonal conditions in the U.S. . . . The mean annual runoff in the arid Southwest is .25 to 10 inches per year or 1-40% of annual precipitation, while the mean annual streamflow in CFS per square mile is very low, often less than 0.1 CSM (de Wiest 1965: 62).

Not only is the amount of irrigation possible related to climate, but the amount which is necessary is related to climatic variation. Olivier in *Irrigation and Climate* (1961: v) has shown, utilizing the Rio Grande as one of his test areas, that:

. . .the ideal quantitative requirements of water on the fields for a crop-soil unit are controlled by climatic and latitude factors and that the average basic needs might therefore be predicted from simple standard meteorological data.

Having substantiated the climatic-subsistence base relationship, I will now turn to the change in population pressure proposition of the explanation. The proposition suggests that not until after 1800 did population pressure on the limited resources of the Rio Grande and Zuñi areas become acute. Although population contact was increasing prior to 1800, at no time did total population (population contact and native population) exceed 50,000. In comparison to the 500,000 plus that was eventually to be supported by the area and imports, it is not unreasonable to suggest that this 10 percent could be supported even given the less sophisticated technology. It is clear that during the "early" part of what Spicer (1962: 295,302) calls the "Spanish program," the Pueblos were able to support not only themselves, but the entire Spanish superstructure including missionaries, encomenderos, and even intermittent tax payments to the Spanish viceroy.

Usually three days' work for the missionary was the rule, with some pressure from the latter to work equally regularly on the Indian fields. The work for the mission was strictly supervised by the missionary's appointees, such as the head herdsman and the head plowman, and the missionaries sanctioned whipping for the enforcement of the daily stint of labor. . . . New Mexican encomenderos forced Pueblo Indians to work for them, frequently with no, or very small, compensation and were reported to have disrupted the lives of villagers by interfering in their local affairs.

In stark contrast to this self-supporting but enslaved posture is the image of the Pueblos under BIA rule by the 1850s. The Pueblos as well as the other tribes in the Southwest had become what Spicer (1962: 346) terms "dependent nations." The policy of the government was to make the Indians dependent on land which could not support them, with the United States government undertaking to support them on a ration basis. In the agents' reports to the Commissioner of Indian affairs, there are many pleas for additional aid. For example, the Pueblo agent Graves in 1866 wrote:

As will be noticed, I relieved the urgent wants of the Pueblo Indians of Isleta, Santo Domingo, and Santa Ana. These people will require further assistance by the way of food from the first of May... (Graves 1866:134).

He requested a $20,000 appropriation for relief and education.

In addition, there is a continual problem of land encroachment during this era. This manifestation of increasing population pressure is not surprising, for it is within the following national context that it took place.

Congress, no longer hampered by the fearsome slave owners, passed the Homestead Act (1862) offering free farms to all adult citizens and to aliens who had their declaratory papers, thus, in effect inviting the laborers of the Old World and the farmers and mechanics of the East, women no less cordially than men, to come and share the bounties of nature, and setting in motion a swift partition of riches which, before twenty years had elapsed transferred over fifty million acres from the national domain to private ownership.... Within twenty-five years after the passage of the Homestead Act all the best land between the Mississippi and the mountains, available under that statute, had been staked out and transferred to private ownership, except the rich Indian Territory occupied by the red man.... Already a clamor had been heard in Washington for the removal of this barrier to the march of Manifest Destiny (Charles and Mary Beard 1930: 127, 143).

Warny, the Pueblo Indian Agent, in his report for 1872 not only asks for appropriations but for the settlement of land controversies with squatters in favor of the Indians. The continuation of this problem may be noted in the later BIA reports and in the 1890 special census report, in which a census agent notes the fear of the 600 members of a pueblo in taking action against one squatter.

With the addition of acute population pressure on scarce resources, as documented above, there developed differential access to the resource base and its products. There was a substantial difference between the economic levels of the Anglo and Spanish-American populations, and that of the Indian population. This difference was not only the result of limited and failing economic development programs created by the contacting cultures, but also the rapid change in Mexican and Anglo economies. Spicer (1962: 540) clearly comments on this change in his chapter of *Cycles of Conquest* entitled "Economic Integration."

With increasing acceleration, the basis and nature of agriculture underwent profound changes, shifting from small- to large-scale production with corresponding changes in economic organization. At the beginning of these changes the Indian communities were operating at a low level of production on a very small scale; as the Mexicans and Anglos rapidly outstripped them the gap between Indian and White economic life widened.

He documents the systematic appropriation not only of land, but of water resources by the dominant Anglo society.

Finally, the United States government attempted to diminish the economic gap.

...faced with the problem of increasing populations on limited and (with the exception of the Eastern Pueblos) generally marginal farm lands, the Indian Bureau sought to develop new land through irrigation and to improve production through the introduction of better crops and farm machinery.... The conception behind the work was to entrench the small subsistence type of farming.... The chief exception to this kind of low level production on subsistence farms was to be found among the Eastern Pueblos and the Zuñi, where Indian Bureau efforts resulted in a reconsolidation of the old Pueblo subsistence farming...with some slight production of a few crops for the local market among the Eastern Pueblos (Spicer 1962: 544-45).

This policy resulted by the 1940s in a mixture of off-reservation labor, welfare, grazing, and agriculture as the income basis for most of the Pueblos. The importance of the exception of the Eastern Pueblos and Zuñi will soon become apparent in terms of our data.

Given the differential access to resources following ethnic lines in the post-1800 period, we would expect that the Indians would be most affected by the increasing scarcity of resources. The continuing increase of the non-Indian population, while Indian population fluctuates (Figs. 4 and 5) validates this expectation. The fact that this fluctuation correlates to economic productivity in the agricultural sector as reflected by climatic potential is not surprising. Since the Pueblos are at the carrying capacity of their diminished resources (they even have to appeal for governmental aid), minor changes in the carrying capacity, such as those caused by climate, will have noticeable effects on population. These effects are far greater than those that would have resulted from equal climatic changes in the pre-1800 disequilibrium period.

In addition, one finds that individually Taos, Santo Domingo, and Zuñi are the three pueblos which most correlate with climate in the post-1800 period. Dozier has suggested that these are the most conservative pueblos. If they have most closely followed the traditional pattern of relying upon agriculture for their economic base and if, as Spicer claims, the agricultural development was most successful in the Eastern Pueblos and Zuñi, these results are exactly what one would expect. In other words, population would most clearly correlate with agricultural production as dictated by climatic potential for these pueblos.

The propositions which have been substantiated will be summarized as follows:

1. There is a relationship between climate and population for the Rio Grande Pueblos taken as a group after 1800, but not prior to 1800.

2. Santo Domingo is the only pueblo which shows a direct correlation between climate and population at a 95 percent significance level throughout its entire history within the scope of this paper.

3. Taos, Santo Domingo, and Zuñi after 1800 all show a direct relationship between climate and population which is not due to chance. Dozier has noted that these three pueblos are the most conservative, and Spicer that agriculture was most successful under BIA development. One is justified in generating two hypotheses to be tested further: (a) the more conservative a pueblo is socially and economically, the more important climate is in limiting population size, and (b) Santo Domingo has been conservative for a longer period of time than has Taos, Zuñi, or the other pueblos.

4. Hypothesis 3 has been shown valid; the evidence does not support any of the others. The primary hypothesis — as population contact increases, the importance of climate as a determinant of Pueblo native population decreases — has been rejected. In fact, it would appear that the opposite is the case: as population contact increases, the importance of climate as a determinant of Pueblo population increases.

5. I have suggested a possible explanation based upon the increase of population contact and the resultant strain on limited resources. This explanation has been substantiated by ethnohistorical data and the correlation of Taos, Santo Domingo, and Zuñi's populations individually with climate.

CHAPTER 4
THE MIGRATORY RESPONSE

Introduction, Hypotheses, Assumptions

What was the Pueblo response to contact? As previously noted, there were several contacting cultures which impinged upon the Pueblos. It is possible to conceptualize these contacts, whether aboriginal, Spanish, Mexican, or Anglo, as vectors. These vectors have variable direction and force, and thus differentially affected each pueblo and the Pueblo area in general.

The Spanish and Mexican contact periods may be characterized as a generally increasing force, with one exception, originating in the south and directed northward. This exception dates from 1680 to approximately 1775 (Spicer 1962). First, the Pueblo revolt made peaceful contact impossible, and then the Apache Corridor made travel between Sonora and Santa Fe dangerous without a full military escort. Anglo contact beginning in the 1840s from the East, directed westward, did not result in large scale immigration until the passage of the Homestead Act and the completion of the Atchison, Topeka, and Santa Fe Railroad (Charles and Mary Beard 1930).

Before turning to a more detailed discussion of our assumptions, I suggest the following set of hypotheses:

1. In response to Mexican and Spanish encroachment and contact from the south, there was Pueblo population movement to the north.

2. In response to Anglo encroachment and contact from the East, there was Pueblo population movement to the West.

3. Since the primary contacting community was Santa Fe (founded 1610) or Albuquerque (founded 1706), there was a Pueblo response to redistribute population so that distance from the contacting community was maximized and contact minimized.

In order to test these hypotheses, it will be necessary to make the following assumptions. (a) Goodrich (1936) has shown that areas of low-standard living and low employment tend to be areas of net out migration, while areas of high-standard living and high employment tend to be areas of net in migration. We will assume that the general standard of living and employment rate of all the Pueblos, based upon social, occupational, technological, and ecological similarities, are broadly equal. (b) If two areas are in different economic regions, Folger (1953) has shown that the relationship between distance migrated and the number of migrants may be different from the relationship within an economically integrated area. We assume that the Pueblo area is an economically integrated area. (c) The rate of migration has been shown by Bogue and Hagood (1953) to vary with the type of community or origin and destination, the direction of migration, and the age and other characteristics of the migrant. Also, it is clear that a high proportion of all migration streams is a flow between communities of the same type, for instance, urban to urban, or farm to farm (Bogue, Shryock, and Hoermann 1957). We assume that all the pueblos are of the same order in terms of type of community, and that Santa Fe and Albuquerque are of a different order. (d) The size, direction, and net effects of migration streams are not invariable in time or place, but are reasonably sensitive to social and economic changes occurring in the various communities of origin and destination (Bogue, Shryock, and Hoermann 1957). However, the regional pattern of net migration tends to remain constant for at least several decades, reflecting the continued action of a set of redistributive forces (Shryock and Eldridge 1947). On the basis of these tested hypotheses, we can assume that major trends in migration pattern last for at least two or three decades. (e) We will also assume that the nineteen existing pueblos are representative of all the pueblos with regard to migration forces. In other words, the major forces causing trends in migration patterns have acted upon the nineteen existing pueblos in the same way they have acted upon all the pueblos. (f) We are assuming that certain population checks, such as disease and warfare, which are not affecting the total population equally, originate in and are perhaps caused by the contacting culture. For example, it is not unreasonable to assume that a smallpox epidemic spread from a contact community such as Santa Fe to the various pueblos in a pattern similar to a chain reaction.

Methodology

The methodology for testing these hypotheses is simple. First, I examined my data and culled out the population data for all the years in which I had information on my total sample of nineteen pueblos (Table 8). I calculated each population as a percentage of the annual total population in order to

compensate for the trends which were occurring to the total population (Table 9). Third, I tabulated the increase or decrease in percentages over time for each pueblo. A plus between two dates indicates that a greater portion of the total Pueblo population was living at a given pueblo at the later date than at the earlier date. A minus indicates that a smaller portion of the total population was living at an individual pueblo at the later date than at the earlier date. A zero means no change. Finally, I arranged the pueblos and the data on a south to north axis by distance from Santa Fe, and an east to west axis by distance from Albuquerque (Tables 10, 11, 12, and 13 respectively).

TABLE 8
The Population of The Pueblos Arranged on a South to North Axis Through Time

South Date	Isleta	Ácoma	Laguna	Zuñi	Sandía	San Felipe	Santa Ana	Zía	Santo Domingo	Jémez
1760	304	1052	600	664	291	458	404	568	424	373
1790	410	820	668	1935	304	532	356	275	650	485
1797	603	757	802	2716	116	282	634	262	1483	272
1850	751	367	749	1294	241	800	339	124	666	365
1860	440	523	929	1300	217	360	316	115	262	650
1889	1037	582	970	1547	150	501	264	113	930	474
1900	1035	492	1077	1525	81	515	228	115	771	452
1910	956	691	1472	1667	73	502	219	109	817	449
1950	1051	1376	1655	2564	150	721	285	145	978	789

TABLE 9
The Population of The Pueblos Expressed as a Percentage Arranged on a South to North Axis

South Date	Isleta	Ácoma	Laguna	Zuñi	Sandía	San Felipe	Santa Ana	Zía	Santo Domingo	Jémez
1760	3.79	13.13	7.49	8.29	3.63	5.72	5.04	7.09	5.29	4.65
1790	4.60	9.21	7.50	21.72	3.41	5.97	4.00	3.09	7.30	5.45
1797	5.87	7.37	7.81	26.44	1.13	2.75	6.17	2.55	14.44	2.65
1850	9.42	4.60	9.39	16.23	3.02	10.03	4.25	1.56	8.35	4.58
1860	6.55	7.78	13.83	19.35	3.23	5.36	4.70	1.71	3.90	9.67
1889	12.57	7.05	11.75	18.74	1.82	6.07	3.20	1.37	11.27	5.74
1900	12.86	6.11	13.38	18.95	1.01	6.40	2.83	1.43	9.58	5.62
1910	10.94	7.90	16.84	19.07	.84	5.74	2.51	1.25	9.35	5.14
1950	8.76	11.46	13.79	21.36	1.25	6.01	2.37	1.21	8.15	6.57

Discussion of the Results

Given these assumptions, one would expect:

1. On the basis of hypothesis 1 (the south to north migration), that the proportion of the total population living in the south would decrease, and the proportion living in the north would increase.

2. On the basis of hypothesis 2 (the east to west migration), that the proportion of the total population living in the east would decrease and the proportion living in the west would increase.

3. On the basis of hypothesis 3 (the migration away from contact communities), that the proportion of the total population living closest to Santa Fe or Albuquerque would decrease, and that the proportion living farthest from these contact communities would increase.

An inspection of the tables shows that Table 10 has a high cluster of pluses for the first seven pueblos and a medium cluster for the rest. This distribution is not what is expected from hypothesis 1, for it shows that the southern pueblos are increasing rather than decreasing in their proportions of the total population. In addition, Table 11 has a large clustering of minuses for the first seven pueblos which gradually decreases for the middle five pueblos, and becomes a large clustering of pluses in the last seven pueblos. This distribution is expected on the

Cochití	Tesuque	Nambé	San Ildefonso	Pojoaque	Santa Clara	San Juan	Picurís	Taos	
450	232	204	484	99	257	316	328	505	
720	138	155	240	53	134	260	254	518	
505	155	178	251	79	193	202	251	531	
254	119	107	319	48	279	568	222	361	
172	97	107	166	37	179	343	143	363	
300	94	80	189	18	187	373	120	324	
247	80	81	137	12	222	422	95	462	
237	80	88	114	16	243	388	104	517	
289	145	96	152	2	511	152	99	842	North

Cochití	Tesuque	Nambé	San Ildefonso	Pojoaque	Santa Clara	San Juan	Picurís	Taos	
5.62	2.90	2.55	6.04	1.24	3.21	3.94	4.09	6.30	
8.08	1.55	1.74	2.69	.60	1.50	2.92	2.85	5.82	
4.92	1.51	1.73	2.44	.77	1.88	1.97	2.44	5.17	
3.19	1.49	1.34	4.00	.60	3.50	7.12	2.78	4.53	
2.56	1.44	1.59	2.47	.55	2.66	5.10	2.13	5.40	
3.64	1.14	.97	2.29	.22	2.27	4.52	1.45	3.93	
3.07	.99	1.01	1.70	.15	2.76	5.24	1.18	5.74	
2.71	.92	1.01	1.30	.18	2.78	4.44	1.19	5.91	
2.41	1.21	.80	1.27	.02	4.26	1.27	.82	7.02	North

TABLE 10
The Change in The Distribution of Pueblo Population Through Time
Arranged on a South to North Axis

South Date	Isleta	Ácoma	Laguna	Zuñi	Sandía	San Felipe	Santa Ana	Zía	Santo Domingo	Jémez
1760										
1790	+	–	+	+	–	+	–	–	+	+
1797	+	–	+	+	–	–	+	–	+	–
1850	+	–	+	–	+	+	–	–	–	+
1860	–	+	+	+	+	–	+	+	–	–
1889	+	–	–	–	–	+	–	–	+	–
1900	+	–	+	+	–	+	–	–	–	–
1910	–	+	+	+	–	–	–	–	–	–
1950	–	+	–	+	+	+	–	–	–	+

TABLE 11
The Change in The Distribution of Pueblo Population Through Time Arranged on an East to West Axis

East Date	Taos	Picurís	Nambé	Tesuque	Pojoaque	San Juan	San Ildefonso	Santa Clara	Cochití	Santo Domingo
1760										
1790	–	–	–	–	–	–	–	–	+	+
1797	–	–	–	–	+	–	–	+	–	+
1850	–	–	–	–	–	+	+	+	–	–
1860	+	–	–	–	–	–	–	–	–	–
1889	–	–	–	–	–	–	–	–	+	+
1900	+	–	–	–	–	–	–	+	–	–
1910	–	–	0	–	–	–	–	+	–	–
1950	+	–	–	+	–	–	–	+	–	–

TABLE 12
The Change in The Distribution of Pueblo Population Through Time
Arranged by Increasing Distance From Santa Fe

Date	Tesuque	Nambé	Pojoaque	San Ildefonso	Santa Clara	Cochití	San Juan	Santo Domingo	San Felipe	Picurís
Nearest to Santa Fe										
1760										
1790	–	–	–	–	–	+	–	+	+	–
1797	–	–	+	–	+	–	–	+	–	–
1850	–	–	–	+	+	–	+	–	+	–
1860	–	–	–	–	–	–	–	–	–	–
1889	–	+	–	–	–	+	–	+	+	–
1900	–	+	–	–	+	–	+	–	+	–
1910	–	0	–	–	+	–	–	–	–	–
1950	+	–	–	–	+	–	–	–	+	–

[70]

Cochití	Tesuque	Nambé	San Ildefonso	Pojoaque	Santa Clara	San Juan	Picurís	Taos	
+	–	–	–	–	–	–	–	–	
–	–	–	–	+	–	–	–	–	
–	–	–	+	–	–	–	–	–	
–	–	–	–	–	–	–	–	+	
+	–	–	–	–	–	–	–	–	
–	–	+	–	–	+	+	–	–	
–	–	0	–	–	+	–	–	+	
–	+	–	–	–	+	–	–	+	North

San Felipe	Sandía	Santa Ana	Isleta	Zía	Jémez	Laguna	Ácoma	Zuñi	
+	–	–	+	–	+	–	+	–	
–	–	+	+	–	–	–	–	+	
+	+	–	+	–	+	+	+	–	
–	+	+	–	+	+	+	–	+	
+	–	–	+	–	–	–	+	–	
+	–	–	+	–	–	–	+	+	
–	–	–	–	–	–	–	–	+	
+	+	–	–	–	+	+	+	+	West

Santa Ana	Sandía	Jémez	Zía	Taos	Isleta	Laguna	Ácoma	Zuñi	
									Farthest from Santa Fe
–	–	+	–	–	+	–	+	+	
+	–	–	–	–	+	–	–	+	
–	+	+	–	–	+	+	+	–	
+	+	+	+	+	–	+	–	+	
–	–	–	–	–	+	–	+	–	
–	–	–	–	+	+	–	+	+	
–	–	–	–	+	–	–	–	+	
–	+	+	–	+	–	+	+	+	

[71]

TABLE 13
The Change in The Distribution of Pueblo Population Through Time
Arranged by Increasing Distance From Albuquerque

Date	Isleta	Sandía	Santa Ana	San Felipe	Zía	Santo Domingo	Jémez	Cochití	Laguna	Ácoma
Nearest to Albuquerque										
1760	+	–	–	+	–	+	+	+	–	+
1790	+	–	+	–	–	+	–	–	–	–
1797	+	+	–	+	–	–	+	–	+	+
1850	–	+	+	–	+	–	+	–	+	–
1860	+	–	–	+	–	+	–	+	–	+
1889	+	–	–	+	–	–	–	–	–	+
1900	–	–	–	–	–	–	–	–	–	–
1910	–	+	–	+	–	–	–	–	+	+
1950										

TABLE 14
Z Values for Pueblos Arranged on an East to West Axis

East Date	Taos– Picurís	Picurís– Nambé	Nambé– Tesuque	Tesuque– Pojoaque	Pojoaque– San Juan	San Juan– San Ildefonso	San Ildefonso– Santa Clara	Santa Clara– Cochití	Cochití– Santo Domingo
1760	8520.6	2581.5	7303.7	3544.4	.3	17701.9	28793.5	4118.6	29444.4
1790	6768.1	1518.9	3300.9	1123.7	.1	7222.2	7444.4	3435.9	72222.2
1797	6856.0	1723.7	4257.7	1189.7	.1	5868.3	11213.7	3470.0	115573.3
1850	4122.5	916.4	1965.0	881.5	.3	20971.3	20602.1	2523.7	26105.5
1860	2670.2	590.3	1601.7	553.9	.1	6590.0	6878.2	1096.4	6954.3
1889	2000.0	370.4	1160.5	261.1	.1	8159.4	3181.2	1997.9	43055.6
1900	2257.7	296.9	1000.0	148.1	.0	6691.4	7040.2	1952.7	29338.4
1910	2765.8	353.1	1086.4	197.5	.1	5119.4	6412.5	2051.0	29381.0
1950	4238.0	366.6	2148.1	44.75	.0	2674.0	17979.6	5259.2	43617.6

TABLE 15
Z Values for Pueblos Arranged by Increasing Distance From Santa Fe

Date	Tesuque– Nambé	Nambé– Pojoaque	Pojoaque– San Ildefonso	San Ildefonso– Santa Clara	Santa Clara– Cochití	Cochití– San Juan	San Juan– Santo Domingo	Santo Domingo– San Felipe	San Felipe– Picurís
Nearest to Santa Fe									
1760	7303.7	4875.0	11091.6	28793.5	4118.6	4114.6	3648.8	22475.9	2243.5
1790	3300.9	1901.6	2944.4	7444.4	3435.9	5416.7	4602.4	40023.1	2018.0
1797	4257.7	3255.1	4590.0	11213.7	3476.0	2951.7	8158.1	48403.5	1057.0
1850	1965.0	1888.9	3544.4	20602.1	2523.7	4174.5	10302.0	61666.6	2652.3
1860	1601.7	916.4	1421.6	6878.2	1096.4	1707.1	2447.3	10916.6	768.8
1889	1169.5	333.4	787.5	8181.2	1997.9	3237.8	9446.9	53927.1	397.8
1900	1000.0	225.0	380.5	7040.2	1952.7	3016.0	8860.6	45956.6	730.7
1910	1036.4	325.9	422.2	6412.5	2051.0	2660.8	8632.8	47469.2	779.7
1950	2148.1	44.5	70.3	17979.6	5259.2	1271.1	4048.4	81613.2	1066.0

Tesuque	San Ildefonso	Santa Clara	Pojoaque	Nambé	San Juan	Picurís	Taos	Zuñi
									Farthest fron. Albuquerque
–	–	–	–	–	–	–	–	+
–	–	+	–	–	–	–	–	+
–	+	+	–	–	+	–	–	–
–	–	–	–	–	–	–	+	+
–	–	–	–	–	–	–	–	–
–	–	+	–	+	+	–	+	+
–	–	+	–	0	–	–	+	+
+	–	+	–	–	–	–	+	+

Santo Domingo— San Felipe	San Felipe— Sandía	Sandía— Santa Ana	Santa Ana— Isleta	Isleta— Zía	Zía— Jémez	Jémez— Laguna	Laguna— Ácoma	Ácoma— Zuñi
22475.9	7712.8	6803.5	3344.6	3997.0	32695.1	4144.4	41746.0	9511.5
40023.1	9359.3	6263.0	3974.9	2610.0	20582.6	5999.6	36227.5	21605.4
48403.5	1893.1	4256.0	10411.3	3657.1	10997.5	4039.7	40153.0	27995.8
61666.6	11157.4	4728.0	6933.3	2155.6	6984.6	5062.7	18180.1	6466.5
10916.6	4520.8	3968.2	3786.5	1171.3	11535.4	11182.5	32134.6	9257.9
53927.1	4349.0	2291.6	7455.6	2712.5	8265.7	8514.4	37337.3	12259.7
45956.6	2414.1	1068.8	6426.5	2755.2	8021.6	9014.9	35045.2	10216.5
47469.2	2120.7	925.2	5701.6	2412.2	7552.6	12239.4	67272.0	15689.9
81613.2	6258.7	2474.0	8157.3	3527.7	17655.1	24181.4	50613.8	48040.1 West

Picurís— Santa Ana	Santa Ana— Sandía	Sandía— Jémez	Jémez— Zía	Zía— Taos	Taos— Isleta	Isleta— Laguna	Laguna— Ácoma	Ácoma— Zuñi
									Farthest from Santa Fe
1804.4	6803.5	3350.1	32695.1	2951.0	1225.4	4691.4	41746.0	9511.5
1231.3	6263.0	4450.6	20582.6	1465.5	1675.2	7044.2	36227.5	21605.4
2166.9	4256.0	973.8	10997.5	1431.3	2555.8	12438.4	40153.0	27995.8
1024.8	4728.0	2715.0	6984.6	460.5	2164.0	14467.6	18180.1	6466.5
615.3	3968.2	4353.4	11535.4	429.5	1274.9	10513.4	32134.6	9257.9
431.3	2291.6	2194.4	8265.8	376.7	2681.9	25871.7	37337.3	12259.7
294.9	1068.8	1130.0	8021.6	546.6	3816.8	28670.1	35045.2	10216.5
310.1	925.2	1011.6	7552.6	579.7	3945.2	36194.2	67272.0	15684.9
384.2	2474.0	3652.7	17655.1	1256.1	7063.7	44737.8	50613.8	48040.1

basis of hypothesis 2 for it represents an east-to-west increase in the proportions of total population. Similarly, the data of Table 12 substantiate hypothesis 3 for Santa Fe, and those in Table 13 suggest we reject the hypothesis for Albuquerque.

It might be argued that these results are not caused by contact, but by the "naturally expected migration" which results between any two communities as a simple concomitant of their existence. Historically, it is difficult to determine the migration from specific pueblos to other pueblos for specific years, and almost impossible to determine which part of these migrations were caused by contact and which by other causes. However, Zipf (1949) has argued on the basis of gravity models that the above "natural" amount of migration between any two areas is directly proportional to the product of the population of the two areas, and inversely proportional to the distance between them, i.e., $Z = P1\ P2/d$ where Z is the proportionality factor related to migration,

P1 is the population of a pueblo
P2 is the population of a second pueblo
d is the distance between them.

First, once again the data must be arranged on the east-west axis and by distance from Santa Fe. If "naturally expected migration" rather than contact or other outside stimuli caused the postulated migrations, we would expect: (a) large values of Z in the east and near Santa Fe diminishing toward the west and the further one is from the contact community, or (b) a reasonably constant Z throughout both sequences. The fact that Z arranged in these sequences shows neither of the expected consistent patterns in either sequence (Tables 14, 15) means that the distribution of population cannot be explained simply by "naturally expected migration" between the communities.

It is possible to interpret these results in more than one way. For example, in order to test these hypotheses, I assumed that migration took place primarily between communities of similar type. If we relax this assumption, it is possible to explain the results of Table 18 not by a Pueblo population migration away from Santa Fe, but by the greater assimilation of the geographically closer populations by the contact community. Dozier favors this interpretation. In a sense, this interpretation is the same as our hypothesis, but examined from a different frame of reference. We suggested that the Pueblo population was redistributed away from Santa Fe by migration in order to minimize contact. The other interpretation would suggest that the Pueblo population was redistributed away from Santa Fe by greater assimilation of closer Pueblo populations. The two differ in cause, but not in results, and are not mutually exclusive. What we may be seeing is the result of both processes.

In conclusion, the Spanish and Mexican contact (the south-north vector) did not result in Pueblo population migration to the north. Moreover, along the east-west axis there is considerable evidence to support a Pueblo population migration from the east to the west. This migration could be a response during the later part of the period to Anglo contact pressure from the east, but it does not explain the early part of this trend. Third, there was a redistribution of population away from Santa Fe, the result of migration, assimilation, or both, depending upon the interpretation. Fourth, there is no relationship between Albuquerque and the changing population distribution, and finally, it is impossible to explain the changing distribution by "natural migration streams."

CHAPTER 5
RESIDENTIAL AREA AND AGRICULTURE
A CONTEMPORARY PERSPECTIVE

I have discussed aspects of Pueblo population, contacts, and climate through a considerable length of time. However, the analysis has been restricted to an ecological frame of reference. We have not considered the Pueblos in comparison to the important geographic and demographic processes affecting society as a whole.

In this broader perspective, the total population of the Pueblos makes up one-hundredth of one percent of the national population, and they own only five-hundredths of one percent of the 3,615,211 square miles which comprise the fifty states. If we utilize one of the common typologies (Brush 1953) which have been developed to describe modern United States settlement systems, the Pueblos are seen as a structural anomaly. Brush defines a hamlet as:

1. at least four active residences of which two are not farmhouses,

2. at least six active functional units,

3. a minimum of five buildings actively used by human beings,

4. five or more residential structures or buildings used for commercial or cultural purposes clustered within one quarter of a square mile,

5. one to nine retail or service units, often including service stations, grocery stores, taverns, and churches.

Villages meet all the criteria of hamlets plus:

1. a larger commercial nucleus from ten retail or service units, often including telephone exchanges, lumber and hardware stores, postal delivery, banking facilities, and livestock and livestock feed retail outlets,

2. high schools in approximately one half of the villages,

3. usually incorporated.

Towns meet all of the criteria previously mentioned, and include the following specialized services:

1. at least fifty retail units, thirty of which are types other than groceries, taverns, and filling stations,

2. high schools and the medical and legal services are almost universally represented,

3. an economy based upon servicing itself and the surrounding rural population.

The pueblos are economically closer to the hamlets, having few full-time retail outlets, partially a result of governmental control and the historic institution of the Indian trader. However, in terms of population size and settlement criteria, many of the pueblos would qualify as villages and towns. For example, the 1960 census includes Zuñi as a settlement of 2500+, thus deeming it important enough for separate analysis. (The other pueblos come under miscellaneously lumped categories — either urban or rural — depending upon the exact criteria being used.)

The rural-urban relationship, utilizing the term "urban" in its broadest sense to mean any hamlet or larger concentration of people, has been affected by several processes. Most important has been the rural to urban migration or what Lewis Mumford has called the "urban implosion." The proportion of our population which is dependent on agriculture for a living has decreased since 1900 — 30 percent in 1900, 12.5 percent in 1950, and 8.6 percent in 1960 (Dickenson 1964). Secondarily, there has been a tendency for concentration — the subdivision of urban settlements into functionally specialized areas. One need only note the increasing complex of zoning laws in settlements of village size or larger which has developed over the last fifty years. Third, in comparison to the centripetal forces of concentration and centralization, there has developed a centrifugal force, partially as a result of better transportation, which is causing people and institutions to migrate from high-population density areas into more rural areas. In the urban setting, this movement has been manifested by the development of residential suburbs and industrial "parks," while in the more rural setting it has resulted in the utilization of non-contiguous lands by a single household and the opening of labor markets spatially but no longer temporally distant from the residence.

Due to a lack of published data, it is difficult to determine the effect these processes have had on the pueblos. The governmental agencies who utilize standard criteria, the Census and the BIA, present data in such gross categories as to make impossible an analysis of individual pueblos. The ethnographies differ greatly in date of analysis, data presented, and criteria utilized. However, it is possible to make some limited inferences, even on the basis of incomplete data.

S. D. Aberle in the "Pueblo Indians of New Mexico; Their Land, Economy and Civil Organization," presents data on Indian agricultural land for 1944, listing each pueblo separately. I have quoted her data as column one of Table 16. Column two represents agricultural land in 1969. I calculated these figures from a series of unclassified aerial photographs of the Pueblo areas taken in April, 1969. The photographs were made available by the Strategic Air Command, U.S. Air Force. Examples of the central portions of 20 of the 70 photographs used are presented in Figures 6 to 24. Each original photograph showed 26,740 acres at a scale of 1:30,000. There were three to six overlapping photographs of each pueblo, thus assuring a rather complete coverage of the field patterns.

In order to calculate the actual figures, I made multiple runs (3 or more) with a compensating planimeter and took the average. There were two major problems in the photo interpretation — differentiation of Indian, Anglo, and Spanish fields and the differentiation of recently abandoned fields from fallow fields. In order to differentiate the ownership of the fields, the following criteria were utilized:

1. It was often possible to differentiate on the basis of natural and artificial boundaries which appeared in the photographs.

2. The field configuration for the three groups is usually quite different. Anglo fields tend to be square and rectangular, while the Spanish fields are very long and thin with an irrigation canal running along the short axis. These patterns are related to the differing inheritance rules. Indian fields, although sometimes following either of the above patterns, tend not to be as geometrically perfect, so that triangular and other irregular shapes are often interspersed among the squares and rectangles.

3. The distribution of buildings for the three groups is different. On the Anglo and Spanish fields, farmhouses and outbuildings appear quite regularly. The Indian fields, on the other hand, are large tracts of land either without any buildings or very few. Only in the case of Isleta and Sandía was it impossible to make this differentiation. In order to distinguish recently abandoned fields from fallow fields, each photograph was magnified ten times. If the magnified field showed a considerable amount of irregular overgrowth, it was classified as abandoned; if the overgrowth was regular or if there was no overgrowth, it was classified as fallow. In the cases of Ácoma and Laguna all the fields were abandoned. Dozier noted that most of the population of Ácoma has moved to Acomita, and as with Laguna, the primary source of income has become wage work in a nearby uranium mine.

If one compares Table 16 with Table 17, which presents the amount of farm land in New Mexico and the United States over time, it is clear that the pueblos are following fairly closely certain state and national trends. In all three cases, after a rise during the years of World War II and the Korean war, there is a clear decrease in the amount of agricultural land. For the pueblos, the total decrease of 2452 acres is primarily caused by major decreases at Ácoma, Laguna, and San Ildefonso.

Turning to residential area, Stubbs, in *Bird's Eye View of the Pueblos,* presents a set of aerial photographs (scale 1:3,000) of Pueblo residential areas exclusively. By *residential area,* I mean the area which the village or town covers, thus excluding corrals and agricultural or grazing lands. I made multiple planimeter measurements of Stubbs' photographs to calculate the residential areas; these calculations are presented as column one of Table 18. I did the same with the 1969 aerial photographs; these measurements are found in column two of the same table.

The large increase in these figures between 1944 and 1969 is somewhat deceptive. First, Stubbs' photographs showed such a circumscribed area that some of the outlying houses probably were not shown. Second, the additional areas have considerably lower densities for housing than the central areas

TABLE 16
Agricultural Acreage

Pueblo	1944#	1969*	Change 1944 to 1969
Ácoma	1,391	545**	-1391
Cochití	630	818	+188
Jémez	1,345	2,023	+678
Laguna	1,588	86**	-1588
Nambé	288	344	+56
Picurís	176	430	+254
Pojoaque	35	715	+680
San Felipe	1,419	1,477	+58
San Ildefonso	2,741	674	-2067
San Juan	899	573	-326
Santa Ana	585		-585
Santa Clara	547	559	+12
Santo Domingo	1,644	2,855	+1211
Taos	2,369	1,563	-806
Tesuque	177	387	+210
Zía	312	473	+161
Zuñi	2,833	3,601	+768
Total	18,944	16,492	-2452

*Calculated from aerial photographs by compensating planimeter.
**Abandoned
#S. D. Aberle (1948)

of the pueblos. Thus, we are often adding twice the area of the older pueblo in order to include only a quarter more houses.

It is interesting to note, however, that even with this increase, the Pueblos do not occupy as much residential area as in similar Spanish and Anglo settlements of equivalent population size. This difference is true for all cases with adequate data, as may be seen by examining Table 19, which presents the residential areas and the population of towns in New Mexico over 1,000 in 1960.

In conclusion, from limited data, it appears that the importance of agriculture has been declining in the pueblos as it has in the rest of the nation. The increase in residential area corresponds to the centrifugal forces affecting most settlements in the United States. This increase is not surprising since the population density for Zuñi (186 per acre in 1950) or for San Ildefonso (14 per acre) is greater than that of

Albuquerque, which in 1960 was approximately 6 per acre. Increasing sanitation, a weakening of the traditional social organization, increased ease of transportation are among the causes which have contributed to this decrease in spatial centralization.

TABLE 17
Acreage of Land in Farms

	Millions of Acres	
Date	U. S.*	New Mexico**
1940	1061	38
1945	1142	49
1950	1202	47
1954	1206	49
1959	1183	46
1964	1147	47

*U. S. Statistical Abstract 1968, Table No. 895, p. 594.
**Census of Agriculture 1964, Table No. 2, p. 8.

TABLE 18
Residential Areas of The Pueblos in 1950 and 1969

	Acres	
Pueblo	1950	1969
Ácoma	12	14
Cochití	10	118
Isleta	14	170
Jémez	14	128
Laguna	8	86
Nambé	6	37
Picurís	5	7
Sandía	6	35
San Felipe	10	109
San Ildefonso	10	85
San Juan	7	67
Santa Ana	10	43
Santa Clara	7	95
Santo Domingo	12	61
Taos	14	123
Tesuque	8	42
Zía	11	29
Zuñi	14	293

TABLE 19
Residential Areas and Population
for Places of 1000 Plus in New Mexico*

Places of 1000 + Inhabitants	Residential Area Acres	Population	Places of 1000 + Inhabitants	Residential Area Acres	Population
Alamogordo	8,896	21,723	Los Lunas	576	1,186
Albuquerque	37,248	201,189	Loving	576	1,646
Artesia	1,600	12,000	Lovington	2,368	9,660
Aztec	2,048	4,137	Magdalena	3,904	1,211
Bayard	448	2,327	Mesilla	512	1,264
Belen	1,024	5,031	Milan	4,096	2,658
Bernalillo	448	2,574	Mountainair	640	1,605
Bloomfield	1,728	1,292	Portales	2,048	9,695
Carlsbad	4,928	25,541	Ranchos de Taos	4,492	1,668
Carrizozo	960	1,546	Raton	2,496	8,146
Central	384	1,075	Roswell	8,704	39,593
Clayton	1,984	3,314	Ruidoso	3,136	1,557
Clovis	5,888	23,713	Santa Fe	17,152	33,394
Deming	1,792	2,416	Santa Rosa	1,924	2,220
Española	512	1,976	Silver City	2,880	6,972
Eunice	832	3,531	Socorro	7,488	5,271
Farmington	11,008	23,786	Springer	768	1,564
Fort Sumner	1,088	1,809	Mesilla Park	2,752	4,387
Gallup	2,880	14,089	Tatum	768	1,168
Grants	3,712	10,274	Truth or		
Hagerman	768	1,144	Consequences	6,144	4,269
Hobbs	6,912	26,275	Tucumcari	2,560	8,143
Hurley	704	1,851	Tularosa	1,344	3,200
Jal	3,264	3,051	Vaughn	3,640	1,170
Las Cruces	7,168	29,367			
Las Vegas City	1,664	7,790			
Las Vegas Town	1,472	6,028			
Lordsburg	3,584	3,436			
Los Alamos	3,584	12,584			

*Abstracted from U. S. Dept. of Commerce. Area measurement reports. 1965 "Areas of New Mexico: 1960."

CONCLUSIONS

In this study I have considered several demographic, ecological, and spatial aspects of the New Mexican Pueblos from 1550 to the present. First, I proposed a deductive model relating to climate and native population size. This model was shown inappropriate by the finding that Pueblo population is correlated with climate after 1800 rather than before. The results of the statistical analysis suggest that population pressure caused by Spanish and Anglo immigration into the Rio Grande valley after 1800 produced an acute strain on limited resources. As a result of economic encroachment and ethnically differentiated access to resources, the limiting factor of climate became a constraint upon Indian population. Historical and indirect data corroborate the subsistence difficulties of the Pueblos in the post-1800 period. The economically conservative pueblos were more severely affected.

Second, I analyzed the migratory response of the Pueblos to the Spanish and Anglo immigration. It appears, as might be expected from the above, that the Anglo immigration was more disruptive than the Spanish. There is evidence of an east-to-west migration by the Pueblo population which could not occur as a result of "natural migration" concomitant to differential population size. This vector is the proper one for a response to Anglo migration. There was not, on the other hand, a south-to-north migration, which would be expected as a result of Spanish immigration. It was also shown that Santa Fe was a more disruptive force than Albuquerque in terms of population distribution.

Finally, I examined the effect upon the modern pueblos of the centrifugal and centripetal forces affecting all settlement patterns in the United States today. By utilizing data obtained from aerial photographs, it is possible to show that there is a decreasing dependence on agriculture by an increasing population. Secondly, the national trend toward decentralization of urban and rural settlements is exemplified by the significant increase of residential area in the pueblos. In short, they are in the process of developing suburbs.

REFERENCES

ABERLE, Sophie D.
1948   Pueblo Indians of New Mexico; Their Land, Economy and Civil Organization. *American Anthropological Association, Memoir* No. 70. Menasha.

ADAMS, Eleanor B. (Editor)
1954   Bishop Tamaron's Visitation of New Mexico 1760. *Historical Society of New Mexico Publications in History*, Vol. XV. Albuquerque.

ADAMS, Eleanor B. and Fray Angelico Chavez
1956   *The Missions of New Mexico 1776, A Description by Fray Francisco Atonasio Dominguez*. University of New Mexico Press, Albuquerque.

ALIHAN, Milla Aissa
1964   *Social Ecology: A Critical Analysis.* Cooper Square Publications, Inc., New York.

BANCROFT, Hubert Howie
1889   *The Works of H. H. Bancroft; The History of Arizona and New Mexico 1530-1888.* The History Company, Vol. 17. San Francisco.
1962   *The Works of H. H. Bancroft; The History of Arizona and New Mexico 1530-1888.* Horn and Wallace, Albuquerque.

BANDELIER, Adolf Francis Alphonse
1890   Contributions to the History of the Southwestern Portion of the United States. *Archaeological Institute of America, Papers* (American Series), Vol. 5. Cambridge.

BEARD, Charles and Mary Beard
1930   *The Rise of American Civilization.* Macmillan Company, New York.

BENNETT, John W.
1944   The Interaction of Culture and Environment in the Smaller Societies. *American Anthropologist*, Vol. 46, No. 4, pp. 461-478. Menasha.

BIRDSELL, Joseph Benjamin
1953   Some Environmental and Cultural Factors Influencing the Structuring of Australian Aboriginal Populations. *American Naturalist*, Vol. 86, No. 834, pp. 171-207.
1968   Some Predictions for the Pleistocene Based on Equilibrium Systems Among Recent Hunter-Gatherers. In *Man the Hunter*, edited by Lee and Devore, pp. 229-240. Aldine Publishing Company, Chicago.

BOGUE, D. J. and M. J. Hagood
1953   Subregional Migration in the United States, 1935-40. In *Differential Migration in the Corn and Cotton Belts*, Vol. II. Scripps Foundation Studies in Population Distribution, No. 6. Oxford, Ohio.

BOGUE, D. J., H. S. Shryock and S. A. Hoermann
1957   Subregional Migration in the United States, 1935-40. In *Streams of Migration*, Vol. 1. Scripps Foundation Studies in Population Distribution, No. 5. Oxford, Ohio.

BOULDING, Kenneth E.
  1950   *A Reconstruction of Economics.* John Wiley & Sons, New York.

BROUGHEY, Arthur S.
  1968   *Ecology of Populations.* Macmillan Company, New York.

BRUSH, J. E.
  1953   The Hierarchy of Central Places in Southern Wisconsin. *Geographical Review*, Vol. 43, pp. 380-402.
          New York.

CARROLL, Baily H. and J. Villasona Haggard (Editors)
  1942   *Three New Mexico Chronicles.* The Quivira Society, Albuquerque.

CLARK, John Grahame Douglas
  1952   *Prehistoric Europe: The Economic Basis.* Stanford University Press, Stanford.

CLARKE, L. George
  1954   *Elements of Ecology.* John Wiley & Sons, New York.

CONKLIN, Harold C.
  1955   An Ethnoecological Approach to Shifting Agriculture. *Transactions of New York Academy of
          Sciences*, Series II, Vol. 17, pp. 133-42. New York
  1964   Hanunoo Color Categories. In *Language in Culture and Society*, edited by Dell Hymes, pp. 189-92.
          Harper & Row, New York.

COWGILL, Donald Glen
  1949   The Theory of Population Growth Cycles. *American Journal of Sociology*, Vol. 55, pp. 163-70.
          Chicago.

DAVIS, W. W. H.
  1857   *El Gringo, or New Mexico and Her People.* Harper and Brothers, New York.

de WIEST, Roger J. M.
  1965   *Geohydrology.* John Wiley & Sons, New York.

DICE, Lee R.
  1957   Ecology and Overpopulation. *Scientific Monthly*, Vol. 84, pp. 165-70. Lancaster.

DICKENSON, Robert E.
  1964   *City and Region: A Geographical Interpretation.* Routledge and Kegan Paul, London.

DIXON, W. J. (Editor)
  1965   *BMD Biomedical Computer Programs.* Health Sciences Computing Facility, Department of Preventive
          Medicine and Public Health, School of Medicine, University of California, Los Angeles.

DORN, Harold F.
  1950   Pitfalls in Population Forecasts and Projections. *Journal of the American Statistical Association*,
          Vol. 45, No. 451.

References

DOZIER, Edward P.
    1954   The Hopi-Tewa of Arizona. *University of California Publications in American Archaeology and Ethnology*, Vol. 44, pp. 259-376. Berkeley.
    1961   Rio Grande Pueblos. In *Perspectives in American Indian Culture Change*, edited by E. H. Spicer, pp. 94-186. University of Chicago Press, Chicago.
    1967   *The American Southwest.* MS. unpublished, University of Arizona, Tucson.

DUNCAN, Otis Dudley
    1959   Human Ecology and Population Studies. In *The Study of Population*, edited by Duncan and Hauser, pp. 678-716. University of Chicago Press, Chicago.

DUNCAN, Otis Dudley and Hauser, Phillip Morris (Editors)
    1959   *The Study of Population.* University of Chicago Press, Chicago.

FLANNERY, Kent V.
    1965   The Ecology of Early Food Production in Mesopotamia. *Science*, Vol. 147, pp. 1247-1956. Washington, D.C.

FLANNERY, Kent V. and Michael D. Coe
    1964   Microenvironments and Meso-American Prehistory. *Science*, Vol. 143, pp. 650-54. Washington, D.C.

FOLGER, J.
    1953   Some Aspects of Migration in the Tennessee Valley. *American Sociological Review*, Vol. 18, pp. 253-60. Washington, D.C.

FRAKE, Charles O.
    1964   Diagnosis of Disease Among the Subanun of Mindanao. In *Language in Culture and Society*, edited by Bell Hymes, pp. 193-211. Harper & Row, New York.

FRITTS, H. C.
    1965   Tree-Ring Evidence for Climatic Changes in Western North America. *Monthly Weather Review*, Vol. 93, No. 7, pp. 421-43.

GINI, C.
    1930   The Cyclical Rise and Fall of Population. Reprinted from *Population* by Harris Foundation Lectures, University of Chicago Press, Chicago.

GOODENOUGH, Ward H.
    1964   Language and Property in Truk: Some Methodological Considerations. In *Language in Culture and Society*, edited by Bell Hymes, pp. 185-88. Harper & Row, New York.

GOODRICH, C.
    1936   *Migration and Economic Opportunity.* University of Pennsylvania Press, Philadelphia.

GRAVES, J. K.
    1866   Report of Special Agent J. K. Graves. In *Report of the Commissioner of Indian Affairs for the Year 1866*, pp. 134-36. Government Printing Office, Washington, D.C.

HACKETT, Charles R. (Editor)
    1937   *Historical Documents Relating to New Mexico, Nueva Viscaya and Approaches Thereto, to 1773*, Vol. 3. Carnegie Institution, Washington, D.C.

HALLOWELL, A. I.
  1949   The Size of Algonkian Hunting Territories: A Function of Ecological Adjustment. *American Anthropologist,* Vol. 51, No. 1, pp. 33-35. Menasha.

HODGE, Frederick W.
  1906   Handbook of American Indians North of Mexico. *Bureau of American Ethnology, Bulletin* No. 30. Washington, D.C.

JOHNSTON, Denis F.
  1966   An Analysis of Sources of Information on the Population of the Navaho. *Bureau of American Ethnology, Bulletin* No. 197. Washington, D.C.

KIDDER, Alfred V.
  1958   *Pecos New Mexico: Archaeological Notes.* Papers of the Robert S. Peabody Foundation for Archaeology. Andover.

KROEBER, Alfred Louis
  1939   *Cultural and Natural Areas of Native North America.* University of California Press, Berkeley.

LA FARGE, Oliver
  1959   *Santa Fe, the Autobiography of a Southwestern Town.* University of Oklahoma Press, Norman.

LEE, Richard B. and Irven DeVore (Editors)
  1968   *Man the Hunter.* Aldine Publishing Company, Chicago.

LORIMER, Frank
  1959   The Development of Demography. In *The Study of Population*, edited by Duncan and Hauser, pp. 124-79. University of Chicago Press, Chicago.
  1963   Dynamic Aspects of the Relation of Population to Economic Development. In *Demographic Analysis*, edited by J. J. Spengler and O. D. Duncan. Free Press, Glencoe.

MALTHUS, T. R.
  1789   *Essay on Population.* Reprinted in 1965 by Royal Economic Society. Sentry Press, New York.

MAXON, James C.
  1966   *Effects Upon the Northern Rio Grande Pueblos During the Historic Periods: A Preliminary Survey.* MS. unpublished.

MEGGERS, Betty Jane
  1954   Environmental Limitations on the Development of Culture. *American Anthropologist*, Vol. 56, No. 6, pp. 801-24. Menasha.

MILLER, Merton L.
  1898   *A Preliminary Study of the Pueblo of Taos, New Mexico.* University of Chicago Press, Chicago.

NEWMAN, Marshall T.
  1953   Application of Ecological Rules to the Racial Anthropology of the Aboriginal New World. *American Anthropologist*, Vol. 55, pp. 311-27. Menasha.

References

NOTESTEIN, P. W.
  1945   Population: The Long View. In *Food for the World*, edited by T. W. Schultz, pp. 36-57. University of Chicago Press, Chicago.

ODUM, Eugene P.
  1953   *Fundamentals of Ecology*. W. B. Saunders Co., Philadelphia.

OLIVIER, Henry
  1961   *Irrigation and Climate*. Edward Arnold, London.

OVERPECK, J. G.
  1928   Corn Production in New Mexico. *New Mexico Agricultural Experiment Station Bulletin* 166. Albuquerque.

PARSONS, Elsie Clews
  1925   *The Pueblo of Jémez*. Phillips Academy, Andover.

PEARL, Raymond S.
  1925   *The Biology of Population Growth*. Alfred A. Knopf, New York.

REED, Erik K.
  1964   The Greater Southwest. In *Prehistoric Man in the New World*, edited by J. D. Jennings and Edward Norbeck. University of Chicago Press, Chicago.

SAHLINS, Marshall D.
  1958   *Social Stratification in Polynesia*. University of Washington Press, Seattle.

SANDERS, William
  1968   Hydraulic Agriculture, Economic Symbiosis and the Evolution of Dates in Central Mexico. In *Anthropological Archaeology in the Americas*, pp. 88-107. Theo. Caus' Sons, Brooklyn.

SCHROEDER, A. H. and D. S. Matson
  1965   *A Colony on the Move: Castano de Sosa's Journal, 1590-1*. School of American Research, Santa Fe.

SCHULMAN, E.
  1956   *Dendroclimatic Changes in Semiarid America*. University of Arizona Press, Tucson.

SHRYOCK, H. S. and H. T. Eldridge
  1947   Internal Migration in Peace and War. *American Sociological Review*, Vol. 12, pp. 27-39. Washington, D.C.

SIMPSON, George Gaylord
  1957   *Life: An Introduction to Biology*. Harcourt, Brace & Co., New York.

SMITH, Anne
  1966   New Mexico Indians: Economic, Educational, and Social Problems. *Museum of New Mexico Research Record* No. 1. Santa Fe.

SPICER, Edward D.
  1961   *Perspectives in American Indian Culture Change.* University of Chicago Press, Chicago.
  1962   *Cycles of Conquest: The Impact of Spain, Mexico and the United States on the Indians of the Southwest, 1533-1960.* University of Arizona Press, Tucson.

STEWARD, Julian H.
  1938   Basin-Plateau Aboriginal Sociopolitical Groups. *Bureau of American Ethnology Bulletin* No. 120. Washington, D.C.
  1955   *Theory of Culture Change: The Methodology of Multilinear Evolution.* University of Illinois Press, Urbana.

STUBBS, Stanley A.
  1950   *Bird's-Eye View of the Pueblos.* University of Oklahoma Press, Norman.

THOMPSON, Raymond A.
  1958   Modern Yucatecan Pottery Making. *Memoirs of the Society for American Archaeology,* No. 15.

TURNER, Christy G. II and Laurel Lafgren
  1966   Household Size of Prehistoric Western Pueblo Indians. *Southwestern Journal of Anthropology,* Vol. 22, No. 2, pp. 117-32. Albuquerque.

UCKO, Peter J. and G. W. Dimbleby (Editors)
  1969   *The Domestication and Exploitation of Plants and Animals.* Aldine. Chicago.

U.S. Bureau of the Census
  1841-   *6th Census, 1840* through the *19th Census, 1960.* Government Printing Office, Washington, D.C.
  1963
  1964   *U.S. Census of Agriculture,* Vol. 1. Government Printing Office, Washington.
  1968   *Statistical Abstract of the United States,* 89th edition. Government Printing Office, Washington.

U.S. Department of Interior
  1848-   Reports of the Commissioner of Indian Affairs. In *Annual Report of the Department of the Interior.*
  1968   Government Printing Office, Washington.

U.S. Department of War
  1824-   Reports of the Commissioner of Indian Affairs. In *Annual Reports of the Department of War.*
  1847   Government Printing Office, Washington.

VILLEE, Claude Alvin
  1962   *Biology.* W. B. Saunders, Philadelphia.

VIVIAN, Gordon R.
  1964   Excavations in a 17th Century Jumano Pueblo, Gran Quivira. *National Park Service Archaeological Research Series,* No. 8, Government Printing Office, Washington.

WHITE, Leslie A.
  1935   The Pueblo of Santo Domingo, New Mexico. *Memoirs of the American Anthropological Association,* No. 43. Menasha.
  1942   The Pueblo of Santa Ana. *Memoirs of the American Anthropological Association,* No. 60. Menasha.
  1943   *The Science of Culture: A Study of Man and Civilization.* Grove Press, New York.
  1959   *The Evolution of Culture: The Development of Civilization to the Fall of Rome.* New York, McGraw Hill.

WILLCOX, W. F. (Editor)
  1931   *International Migrations*, Vol. 2. National Bureau of Economic Research, New York.

WILLEY, Gordon Randolph
  1966   *An Introduction to American Archaeology*, Vol. 1, North and Middle America. Prentice-Hall, New Jersey.

YENGOYAN, Aram A.
  1968   Demographic and Ecological influences on Aboriginal Australian Marriage Sections. In *Man the Hunter*, edited by Lee and DeVore, pp. 185-99. Aldine Publishing Co., Chicago.

ZIPF, G. K.
  1949   *Human Behavior and the Principle of Least Effort.* Addison-Wesley Press, Cambridge.

ZUBROW, Ezra B. W.
  1971a   Carrying Capacity and Dynamic Equilibrium in the Prehistoric Southwest. *American Antiquity.* Vol. 36, No. 2, 1971, pp. 127-38. Salt Lake City.
  1971b   *A Southwestern Test of an Anthropological Model of Population Dynamics.* Unpublished Doctoral Dissertation, University of Arizona, Tucson.